D1243178

DANIEL

H. A. IRONSIDE

An Ironside Expository Commentary

DANIEL

H. A. IRONSIDE

Kregel
Academic & Professional

Daniel: An Ironside Expository Commentary

Originally published in 1920. Reprinted in 2005 by Kregel Publications, a division of Kregel, Inc., P.O. Box 2607, Grand Rapids, MI 49501.

Unless otherwise noted, Scripture quotations are from the King James Version of the Holy Bible.

Scripture quotations marked RV are from the Revised Version of the Holy Bible (Church of England, 1885).

Scripture quotations marked WEYMOUTH are from *Weymouth's New Testament in Modern Speech* (1903).

ISBN 0-8254-2912-9

Printed in the United States of America

13 / 5 4 3

CONTENTS

PREFACE

The substance of the exposition in the following pages was first delivered in the form of lectures, at which time shorthand notes were taken that have been revised since and considerably altered by the writer.

Much matter too has been eliminated to reduce the volume, which might have been too large, and thus wearisome to many readers. It is hoped that enough has been retained to give a clear and succinct outline of the teaching of the book of Daniel. By referring from time to time to the chart in Appendix B, the lectures will be considerably simplified.

Critical questions such as authenticity and authorship have not been gone into here, though the present writer has carefully examined practically all that has been urged against receiving this portion of the Holy Scriptures as being in very deed a part of the inspired Word of God. If any reader has doubts or difficulties on these lines, he is referred to the erudite and able expositions and examinations of W. Kelly, Sir Robert Anderson, and Dr. Pusey.

With the prayer that God may be pleased to use this little book to stir up His own people to more devotion to Himself, a more ardent longing for the Coming of our Lord Jesus Christ and our gathering together unto Him, and to the arousing of any who are still in their sins, these lectures are committed to Him who alone can apply them to heart and conscience.

PREFACE TO THE SECOND EDITION

That a second edition of this little book has been called for is cause for unfeigned thankfulness to God, who, I trust, has been pleased to use it in some measure to quicken the faith of His beloved people and to arouse a deeper interest in the study of the prophetic Word.

Since these lectures were first put into print, great and stirring events have transpired. Already one can see the handwriting on the wall that tells of the utter collapse of man's boasted civilization, apart from God, and the rise of the blasphemous powers predicted in Daniel and the Revelation.

In revising the book, very few changes have been made, and those only for the sake of euphony or greater clearness. May the Lord be pleased to continue to use it for His glory and the blessing of souls.

—H. A. IRONSIDE

Brief Analysis of the Chart

The chart accompanying this volume (Appendix B) is a reproduction of a large one, used for the purpose of aiding a clear apprehension of the structure of the book of Daniel when the following lectures were delivered in public.

A little careful study of the diagram will, it is hoped, make plain much that might otherwise be obscure to some who have given but little attention to prophetic teaching.

The first chapter of Daniel, as noted, is introductory and does not itself have a prophetic character, but it pictures, for our instruction, the moral condition suited to enlightenment in regard to the divine ways and counsels emphasizing the need of holiness as a prerequisite to growth in the truth.

Chapters 2–9 are each complete in themselves, giving either actual prophetical instruction or typical lessons of a like character. All, as will be readily observed, culminate in "the time of the end."

What is meant by this last expression will be made clear if it be noted that a parenthetical period in the divine plan is indicated by the broad space between the two heavy lines running right across the chart, near to the center. Everything noted or pictured above the *upper* heavy line represents fulfilled prophecy, or history already accomplished. The line itself, it will be noticed (see the column headed "Chapter 9"), is coincident with the cross of Christ. Below the *second* line we have "The Time of the End." This second line represents the close of the present "church period" at the rapture of the saints, or the Lord's coming to the air. Between the two, we have the whole gospel age, or dispensation of the grace of God, in which He has been pleased to make known "for the obedience of faith," the revelation of the mystery of Christ and the church, "which in other ages was not made known," but was "hid in God" until the rejection and ascension of His beloved Son, followed by the descent of the Holy Spirit to baptize believing Jews and Gentiles into one body, thus securing, for the glory of the Lord Jesus Christ, a heavenly people who will share His throne as the bride of His heart, in the coming age and through eternity.

Now all this was still hidden in the days of Daniel. If the chart were folded so that the two dark horizontal lines touched, the parenthetical period would be hidden, as was the mystery in Old Testament times. With this period covered, we have an outline of what was revealed to Daniel. The great image is then seen to be apparently continuous, and the ten-horned condition of the Beast of chapter 7 follows immediately upon its first rising up.

Chapters 10–12 form one prophecy. The division into past and future occurs between verses 35 and 36 of chapter 11.

Daniel says very little about the kingdom, as his special theme is "the times of the Gentiles." But chapters 2 and 7, and also chapter 12, lead us up to the kingdom, though with little detail regarding it.

If the reader will refer from time to time back to the chart while reading the lectures, it is hoped all obscurity will be removed.

THE NEEDED MORAL CONDITION TO KNOW AND UNDERSTAND GOD'S MIND

Daniel 1

In beginning a series of addresses on this book, I want you first to notice the title of the chart in appendix B—"Outline of the Book of Daniel the Prophet." I call special attention to the name given to Daniel because it is given to him, not by man, but by our Lord Jesus Himself in Matthew 24:15 and Mark 13:14.[1] There we find Him warning His disciples concerning the setting up of "the abomination of desolation spoken of by Daniel the *prophet.*" I emphasize this because it is a common thing with some in our day to deny that there was a prophet Daniel. If you are even moderately familiar with the theories of the destructive "critics," you must know that the book of Daniel was about the first portion of Scripture to which they objected. They declared that it was utterly impossible to credit the idea that Daniel lived in the days of Nebuchadnezzar, Darius, and Cyrus, and yet wrote a book that told of all these world empires before any of them, except the first two, had come into existence. Daniel, these learned teachers tell us, was simply a romancer who lived over two hundred years later and wrote his so-called prophecies after they had all become history.

As a simple believer who owes everything for eternity to what the blessed Christ of God accomplished on Calvary's cross, I prefer to accept His testimony, though it were in opposition to all the wise men of the day. He declared that Daniel was a prophet. He spoke not of Daniel the historian, nor Daniel the romancer, nor Daniel the novelist, but Daniel the prophet—Daniel the man who had been enlightenment by the Spirit of God and, therefore, could speak of the things that were not, as though they were. That is one thing I shall be insisting on in all these lectures. I stand for the full inspiration of all the reputed Word of God and necessarily, therefore, of the book of Daniel.

The first chapter, as noted on the chart, is introductory. It sets forth the moral condition suited to enlightenment in the ways and counsels of God. In it we read of a little company of faithful men maintaining a state of separation to God from evil in a day when everything seemed to be against them, and it appeared as though there was none to whom they could turn for help.

This little company—Daniel, Hananiah, Mishael, and Azariah, four devoted young men—set themselves against all the evil of the kingdom of Babylon. They said, "We will not defile ourselves." These were the men to whom God could communicate His mind. I believe it is important to dwell upon this, because in our own day, alas, in many cases prophetic study has been taken up by very unspiritual persons. If we are going to get the mind of God in studying this book, we must remember that it consists of revelations, deliverances, and visions given to a spiritually minded man who was separated from the iniquity of his day. If we are to understand it, we also need to be spiritually minded and to walk apart from all that is unholy, all that would hinder progress in divine things. We need ever to have before us the words, "Look to yourselves, that we lose not those things which we have wrought, but that we receive a full reward" (2 John 8).

The truth of God is learned through the conscience. This is the reason why the most brilliant men can read the Bible through, over and over again, and never hear the voice of God in it at all. It has been said that "what is one man's meat is another man's poison." The very Word of God may become poison to an unspiritual man if he reads it without being in subjection to God, reads it to find difficulties, and arises from its perusal more confirmed in his unbelief than he was when he sat down to consider it. But, on the other hand, the same book put into the hands of a spiritually minded person—one who has bowed in God's presence, owning his lost condition, who has trusted the Lord Jesus Christ as his Savior, and who is now seeking to live for God and to let his whole life be subject to His Word—that man sits down to the same book and finds it to be food for his soul, building him up on his most holy faith.

If you want enlightenment in divine things, see to it that you walk in the power of an ungrieved Spirit, for "the secret of the LORD is with them that fear him" (Ps. 25:14).

In verses 1 and 2 we find fulfilled the word that God had previously declared by Isaiah, Jeremiah, and others of the prophets would soon take place. For a number of years Jehovah had been sending prophets to the backsliding kings of Judah, warning them that the day of His patience had almost run out and that though Israel had been His chosen people, yet because of their sin, He was going to give them over to the power of their enemies and the land of Palestine was to lie desolate. Singularly enough, as we might consider it, God connects this with their failure to keep the sabbatic year. He had told them when they came into the land that every seventh year must be His. For 490 years they had not kept one sabbatic year. They doubtless thought they would do better by tilling the land annually and that they would be richer as a result of taking their own way. God had told them that if they gave every seventh year to Him they would have abundance in the sixth year to last them until harvest in the eighth year. But they evidently did not believe Him, and they thought to better themselves by their own efforts. Thus, through covetousness—a sin that is eating like a canker among many of God's professed people today—the word of the Lord was ignored and His commandment broken. For 490 years, He seemed to be indifferent to this breach of obedience on their part. He appeared to wink at their sin. But He had taken account of it all. When they, perhaps, thought His law had become as a dead letter, He sent Jeremiah to tell them that now they must go down to Babylon as captives there for seventy years while the land kept Sabbath! They had cheated God out of seventy years, they thought. But He squared the account by giving them into the power of Nebuchadnezzar, king of the Chaldeans, who carried them away to the land of Shinar. There they remained until the seventy years had expired, while the lost Sabbaths were being made up.

It is a very common thing for men thus to forget the claims of God and to suppose that He will never assert Himself. Even saints have been known to fail in this respect. But none ever prospered who ignored the authority of Jehovah in the past, and none can prosper now who forget the obedience due as children to a Father and as redeemed ones to Him who is not only Savior, but Lord. In the world, and even in the church nowadays, we hear a great deal about the rights of the people, but there is One whose rights we do not hear emphasized as often as we should—the rights of our Lord Jesus Christ. Men of the world are utterly indifferent to *His* rights, and saints are only too apt to fall in with the spirit of the times. But a day is fast approaching when God is going to square the account.

Men may not be concerned just now about what is due to Him, but the day is coming when He is going to awake from His seeming slumber, as He tells us in the Psalm 50. Then their proud, haughty knees will have to bow and their tongues confess that Jesus Christ is Lord of all, to the glory of God the Father, when the once-rejected Savior manifests His authority and power. Judah ignored God's rights, and the result was they were sent down to Babylon, as we find in these opening verses.

But there was a second and greater reason still why God chose to give His heritage over to the power of the Chaldeans. For centuries idolatry had been gaining ground among them. They had turned away from Him, the living and true God, to serve the false gods of the heathen. Now Babylon was the home of idolatry, so thither the Jews were sent that they might learn to loathe the idols they had loved. And we find the lesson was well impressed. Ever since the captivity, the Jewish nation, whatever its other sins, has been free from this great evil. Unhappily, they are like the house empty, swept and garnished, from which the evil spirit of idolatry has been driven, but they refused Messiah when He came in lowly grace. So, in the not very distant future, a host of wicked spirits will enter the empty house, and the Jews, save a preserved and delivered remnant, will own and worship the "Man of sin." But of this more later.

The four youths already mentioned were specially distinguished among the rest of their captive brethren. They were taken in charge by the king's orders that they might be trained to administer in state affairs, and fitted for positions of trust and confidence. The name of each of them contains some form of the name of God in Hebrew and indicates their pious ancestry, for in Scripture names have meanings that often help greatly in elucidating the Holy Spirit's mind on a given subject.

All these young men were devoted to Jehovah, as their names imply. But that did not suit the prince of the eunuchs into whose charge they were given, so he gave them new names that indicated their subjection to the Chaldeans, calling Daniel Belteshazzar, and the others Shadrach, Meshach, and Abednego—names that contain the titles of heathen deities—as though he would thus force them to own themselves the subjects of senseless idols. But these labeled men (labeled as servants to heathen gods) stood firmly for the God of Israel and refused to dishonor Him by compliance with a demand that would have rendered them unclean before Him.

The test came. They were to eat of the king's meat, and all that meat was dedicated to idols, making it abhorrent and defiling to a godly Jew. But as the king had given his orders, it might have seemed as though these Hebrews had no choice in the matter. Many, at least, would have argued in this way and said there was no individual responsibility in such a case. Nebuchadnezzar's authority was derived from God. They had only to obey, they might reason, as the Lord Himself had put them in his power. But not thus did Daniel or his young companions view it. They looked upon the king's command as a trial of their faith. Would they keep themselves from the unclean in the land of the idolater? Would they be just as particular about being true to God as if they were in their own land, giving due honor to His Word and seeking to glorify Him by subjection thereto, though captives in the country of the oppressor?

They stood the test in a most marked way, as did the apostles in a later day, who said, "We ought to obey God rather than men" (Acts 5:29). Daniel besought the master of the eunuchs that he would give them pulse—vegetable food—to eat. Fearing the result upon their physical constitutions, he objected, dreading to incur the king's wrath. But the devoted young men pleaded that, at least, an opportunity be given to prove whether they would not thrive as well upon pulse as the rest of the company did upon the king's meat. To this Melzar consented, and the test showed that at the end of ten days Daniel and his three friends were fatter and fairer than any who were fed with the regulation diet. Permission was accordingly given to continue the same fare, and, thus, they were able to maintain a position of separation from the unclean, even in the very home of idolatry.

Now all this might have seemed to many of the Jews a very trivial matter, and some who read the account in our day may also consider it all a mere quibble on the part of Daniel, Hananiah, Mishael, and Azariah. But it brings out a principle of great force and beauty that should appeal to every Christian heart and conscience. Mark you, the only way to go on with God is by being faithful in little things. He who honors the Lord by conscientious adherence to His Word in what some would call minor details is likely to be exercised about greater things. I have heard Christians refer to certain precepts in the Scriptures as nonessentials. But we may rest assured there are no nonessentials in our Bibles. "The words of the Lord are pure words, as silver tried in [the fire], purified seven times" (Ps. 12:6). When people talk of nonessentials in regard to anything concerning which God has revealed His mind, it is well to ask, "Essential or nonessential to what?" If it be a question of the soul's salvation, undoubtedly the one great essential is faith in His blessed Son, whose finished work alone avails to put away sin and procure peace with God. But if it be a question of what is essential to the enjoyment of communion with God—essential to obtaining the Lord's approval at the judgment seat of Christ—then it is well to remember that in everything the believer is sanctified to the obedience of Christ. And it is here that we should seek to imitate Daniel, who had "purposed in his heart" that he would not defile himself.

Paul and Barnabas besought the early Christians to "cleave to the Lord with purpose of heart." It is only thus we will be kept from defilement. Anything that defiles the conscience at once breaks the link of communion with God and hinders our advance in spiritual things. There can be no true progress if there be not care to preserve inviolate this inward monitor. "Holding faith, and a good conscience; which some having put away concerning faith have made shipwreck" (1 Tim. 1:19) is a solemn word worthy of being carefully pondered.

It was because of their carefulness in maintaining a good conscience that these Hebrew young men were given spiritual enlightenment above all the men of their times. They had an understanding in divine mysteries that others failed to enter into, because it remains true in all dispensations that "spiritual things are spiritually discerned" (see 1 Cor. 2:14). God does not commonly impart His secrets to careless men, but to those who are devoted to His interests. He may, in His sovereignty, use even a Balaam or a Caiaphas to utter divine truth, but cases like these are extraordinary. The rule is that "the secret of the LORD is with them that fear him" (Ps. 25:14).

It is of grave importance that we bear this principle in mind in these Laodicean times. We live in days when everything that once was deemed important is looked upon as a matter of indifference, when truth for which myriads of martyrs shed their blood is considered hardly worthy of being contended for—days when the claims of God as set forth in His faithful Word are openly set aside even by those who "call themselves by the name of the Lord" and who profess to owe every-thing to the cross on which the Lord Jesus died. Latitudinarianism is the prevail-ing order, and few ask, with intention to obey, "What saith the Scripture?" Is it any wonder that a host of false teachings is coming in like a flood and thousands on every hand are being swept away from their moorings? A good conscience—that is, a conscience in all things controlled by the Word of God—once put away, shipwreck of the faith is almost certain to follow. It is not a question of shipwreck of faith in Christ, but by putting away a good conscience people make shipwreck of *the* faith.[2] The term *the faith* means "the faith of God's elect," the truth He has revealed, and concerning which Paul wrote, "Holding the mys-tery of the faith in a pure conscience" (1 Tim. 3:9). It is the same as that spoken of by Jude, who writes exhorting believers to "earnestly contend for the faith which was once delivered unto the saints" (Jude 3).

And so we may lay it down as an axiom proven by experience and supported by Scripture that the only way we can advance in the truth is by maintaining a good conscience. Allow one thing in your life unjudged that you know to be contrary to the Word of God, or that you fear is not in line with God's will for you, and you will soon find your spiritual eyes become darkened, your spiritual susceptibilities deadened, and no real progress made in your soul, but rather a steady decline. But where there is faithfulness in separation from that which is opposed to the mind of God, where His Word is allowed to sit in judgment on all your ways, you will learn that "the path of the just is as a shining light, that shineth [brighter and brighter] unto the perfect day" (Prov. 4:18). The Word will illumine each step before you as you take the one already pointed out.

It is written of these four young men that "God gave them knowledge and skill in all learning and wisdom: and Daniel had understanding in all visions and dreams" (Dan. 1:17). In this he reminds us very much of Joseph, who also entered into the secrets of the Lord and who was first characterized by fidelity to God, so that God's smile, God's approbation meant more, was more to him than the smile or the friendship and approval of any human being. And just as it was with Daniel, who came "into favour and tender love with the prince of the eunuchs" (Dan. 1:9), so Joseph, exhibiting the godliness of his life and the transparency of his nature, came into favor with the keeper of the prison. To crown it all, we find God opening his understanding, giving him wisdom in the interpretation of dreams and visions, as here with Daniel.

What a lesson for us—that purity of heart and faithfulness to God come before enlightenment in divine mysteries! If you attempt to reverse these things, you need not be surprised if you fall into all kinds of error. If you try to put knowledge before heart purity, if you try to put a grasp of Scripture truth before conscientious living in the presence of God, you are almost certain to have a fearful fall awaiting you. It is right here that large numbers have failed who may well be a warning to us.

Thus this first chapter of Daniel comes to us as a serious reminder of the necessity of holiness on the threshold of this book of types and prophecies. It reminds us that if we want to go on and learn all that God has revealed in the various chapters following, we need first to stop and ask ourselves, "Am I, personally, right with God? Am I seeking to live so as to honor Him in all my ways?" It is the solemnity of this that I want to press upon my own soul, and upon each one here, as I close this lecture. Oh that both saved and unsaved may consider it well!

If out of Christ, I would affectionately remind you of the danger in which you stand. Later we shall be speaking of woes and sorrows, in the throes of which this poor world will soon be. And is it here that you have your *all?* You are building your hopes for happiness in a wasting scene! Many things which in this book of Daniel are given as prophecy have now become history; many other portions will soon be fulfilled. Dear unsaved one, if you continue in your sins until "the time of the end"—without God and without hope—your sorrows, your anguish, your bitter, bitter woes will be more than tongue can tell. Think of what it will mean for gospel rejecters to be going up and down in this scene after the Holy Spirit has been withdrawn—when Christendom has become completely apostate—when the Word of God is no longer preached—when the saints of God have been called home to heaven—when Antichrist's power shall be supreme, and there shall be a famine, not for bread or for water, but for the hearing of the words of the Lord! All this is just before you, in the near future. You may soon enter upon it, if you do not get right with God. Can you afford to longer trifle with events so momentous and fast hastening on?

And if the Lord should not come in your day, and His judgments upon this guilty world be, in grace, deferred for a little, yet consider that you have soon to pass out of this life and stand before His righteous throne and your own evil record, when it will be forever too late to find a Savior. Flee now, I pray you, to Him who bids the sinful, the weary, the thirsty, and the lost; find cleansing, rest, refreshment, and salvation in Himself, who appeared once "to put away sin by the sacrifice of himself" (Heb. 9:26)—who shall soon "appear the second time," apart from the sin question, to the final salvation of all His own!

In view of all this, may we who are redeemed by His precious blood ever remember the word, "I beseech you therefore, brethren, by the mercies of God, that ye present your bodies a living sacrifice, holy, acceptable unto God, which is your reasonable [or, intelligent] service" (Rom. 12:1). Thus shall we stand, like Daniel and his friends, apart from the world's defiling ways.

THE TIMES OF THE GENTILES: THE GREAT IMAGE

Daniel 2

This second chapter has well been called "the A, B, C of prophecy." I suppose it contains the most complete, and yet the most simple, prophetic picture that we have in all the Word of God. And you will notice that it is in the form of a dream given to a heathen monarch. Nebuchadnezzar was at this time the ruler of the greater part of the known civilized world and of a great deal of that which was given over to barbarism. We speak of this as a world empire, though, of course, in one sense of the word, it was hardly that. There were tribes and nations beyond the outskirts of his dominions that were not subject to Nebuchadnezzar—those upon the northern shores of the Mediterranean Sea, for instance, and portions of southern Egypt and the regions beyond. But God had given him the title to rule over all nations. This authority was given to Nebuchadnezzar because of the rejection of Israel as God's kingdom upon earth. Had they been faithful to God, had they always been obedient to Him, royalty never would have departed from Judah.

But because of their disobedience and their manifold sins, God gave their glory to the stranger, and dominion passed to the Gentiles in the person of

Nebuchadnezzar. This was, in fact, the beginning of the distinctive period designated by the Lord Jesus in Luke 21:24 as "the times of the Gentiles," which will continue until all derived power is overthrown and

> Jesus shall reign where'er the sun
> > Doth his successive journeys run;
> His kingdom spread from shore to shore,
> > Till moons shall wax and wane no more.

In the book of Jeremiah, as also in Kings and Chronicles, we read of Nebuchadnezzar coming up against the land of Palestine in the reign of King Jehoiakim. Though at that time—at least, at the time of his first invasion—he was not the emperor, but his father sat upon the throne of the Babylonian dominion, and Nebuchadnezzar was vice king. But when our chapter opens, he had been reigning alone for two years. The glory of God had departed from Jerusalem, and the people of Judah became captives in the land of Shinar: "By the rivers of Babylon, [they] sat down [and] wept, when [they] remembered Zion" (Ps. 137:1).

Now God was pleased to reveal an outline of His ways to this heathen monarch. We learn from Daniel's address to him that this great king had been concerned about what was coming on the earth. Look at verse 29: "As for thee, O king, thy thoughts came into thy mind upon thy bed, what should come to pass hereafter." Nothing could be more natural. Nebuchadnezzar was the most powerful monarch the world had ever known. As he lay upon his bed that night, he began to ponder and to wonder what would come to pass in after years. He knew he could not stay here forever. He would have to pass away as other potentates had done before him. What would follow? It was not unwise for him to consider these things. Would that all men were more concerned about what the future has in store. The great business of the men of today seems to be just to secure wealth and pleasure for the present life, and the majority seem utterly indifferent about what is to come to pass afterward. Now God has not left us in ignorance as to the future. He has given us the prophetic word to shed light on what is to come. If people were but willing to stop long enough to seriously read His book, in subjection to its holy Author, they would find that in it the whole course of human events, right up to the Great White Throne, has been clearly revealed, so that anyone who earnestly desires it may know the truth of God's ways right on to the end.

Nebuchadnezzar was wiser than many nowadays, for he was exercised in regard to these things. As he lay upon his bed, he had an impressive dream, but in the morning it had gone from him. It still swayed his mind, however. He could not throw it off. He found it impossible to overcome the impression made upon him. Yet, when he tried to recall what it was he had dreamed, he could not do so. So, according to the custom of his times, he sent for his wise men—the soothsayers, astrologers, and magicians. To them he said, "I have dreamed a dream, but it has gone from my mind; and I want you to tell me my dream, and then tell me the interpretation of it."

Miserable charlatans that they were, they pleaded the absurdity and impossibility of this, declaring, what was possibly true enough, that no king or ruler had ever asked anything so difficult of his wise men. They assured the king that if he would but relate the dream, they would explain its meaning. But he declared that if they had skill enough to interpret dreams, they ought to be able to tell him the dream also. He threatened that if after a limited time they did not accede to his demand, they should all be put to death, and not only they, but all the wise men in his kingdom—which, of course, included Daniel.

When Daniel learned of the decree through Arioch the captain of the guard, he went in and besought Nebuchadnezzar to grant a brief respite that he might seek the face of God regarding the matter. Communicating the seriousness of the situation to his three friends, they together made supplication to the God of heaven.

I want you to notice that title—"The God of heaven." Nothing shows the divine source and verbal inspiration of the Scriptures more clearly than the way in which the names and titles of the Deity are used throughout the Bible. Unspiritual and ignorant men have sometimes tried to make capital out of the diversity of divine names, supposing different gods to be meant, and arguing therefrom a piecemeal arrangement of some of the books. But the fact of the matter is that all these names and titles are used in a most exact and careful manner. For instance, in the entire Old Testament, Jehovah is always used in one particular sense and Elohim (God, plural form) in another. When it is the Creator that is brought before us, then we have the Hebrew word *Elohim,* implying the Triune God, now revealed in three persons as Father, Son, and Holy Spirit. When it is a question of God's covenant with His people, of His having to do with the men whom He has made and taken into relationship with Himself, then it is Jehovah. It is not only in Genesis, but throughout the Bible, that this holds good.

Now as to this expression, "The God of heaven," there are three books in the Old Testament where it is used, and one in the New Testament—the Revelation.

The three Old Testament books are Ezra, Nehemiah, and Daniel. All refer, practically, to the same period when God had scattered His people among the nations because of their sins. He had forsaken His throne at Jerusalem. The glory had gone up to heaven, and He was no longer called the Lord of the whole earth. He was now the God of heaven, and, so far as the world is concerned, that is still His title. He will never again be owned as the Lord of the whole earth until the Millennium.

And so Daniel and his friends entreated the God of heaven. He answered their cry and revealed the secret. Then we read, "Daniel blessed the God of heaven." You will notice that we have three things here: first, prayer—"They desired mercies of the God of heaven." Then there is divine ministry—God revealed the thing unto Daniel in a night vision. And the result of that was worship—"They blessed the God of heaven." Where God is speaking, it stirs the hearts of His people and leads them out in worship and praise back to Himself. People have very low ideas about worship nowadays. They talk about worshiping God no matter what religious exercise they may be engaged in. But let us remember that even prayer is not worship, and ministry is not worship. Prayer is asking of God; ministry is when God gives something to man. But when man has asked, and God has given until the heart is full and overflows in adoration back to God, this is worship.

My wife and I stood one day looking down on Niagara Falls. How our hearts were stirred as we watched that mighty cataract pouring its tremendous volume of water over the great cliff unceasingly. But soon we noticed that from below a mist or fine spray rose up that actually reached the point where we stood on the ledge above the Falls. I said to my wife, "This is like worship—God's mighty love and grace pouring down upon us, and then our love and praise rising up and ascending back to Him, the source of all our blessing."

The Father is seeking worshipers, but people have to be born again before they can worship Him. How can a poor guilty sinner, who has never been brought into the family of God, never been converted, be a worshiper in spirit and in truth? Yet we hear often of "public worship," but the fact of the matter is, the public, as such, cannot worship in the Christian sense.

But to turn back to Daniel. He comes in before the king and tells him that he is able to reveal the secret. He makes it plain that it is not through any superior wisdom of his own that he is able to do this, but he tells Nebuchadnezzar, "There is a God in heaven that revealeth secrets, and maketh known to the king Nebuchadnezzar what shall be in the latter days" (v. 28). It was of God that this great king was brought to the end of all human resources. If he had been able to remember his dream, he never would have realized that he had to do with God. He had first to be brought to the end of all human wisdom. He had to learn his own nothingness and ignorance, and the nothingness and ignorance of all his wise men, in order that the matchless wisdom of God might be revealed to him. And the same lesson must be learned by us. If we are ever going to have to do with God, we have to learn the poverty of our own resources first.

Have you ever noticed where the Lord Jesus Christ was crucified? It was at Golgotha—the place of a skull. If you were ever saved, you began at the place of a skull. That is not very nice for human pride, for it is the place of death and the end of all human wisdom. You cannot reason it out. All the wise men of the earth cannot teach it you. You have to be brought to the place of an empty skull—the helplessness of death—where you realize that God is writing confusion on all the wisdom of this world. And so this great king had to be brought to the place where he learned that "man's extremity is God's opportunity." Then it was that the God of heaven, through His prophet, revealed to him the dream and its interpretation. Daniel says:

> Thou, O king, sawest, and behold a great image. This great image, whose brightness was excellent, stood before thee; and the form thereof was terrible. This image's head was of fine gold, his breast and his arms of silver, his belly and his thighs of brass, his legs of iron, his feet part of iron and part of clay. Thou sawest till that a stone was cut out without hands, which smote the image upon his feet that were of iron and clay, and brake them to pieces. Then was the iron, the clay, the brass, the silver, and the gold, broken to pieces together, and became like the chaff of the summer threshingfloors; and the wind carried them away, that no place was found for them: and the stone that smote the image became a great mountain, and filled the whole earth. (vv. 31–35)

At once the king recognized the fact that it was indeed the dream he had forgotten. Daniel then proceeded with the interpretation. The image properly represents the whole period of the times of the Gentiles. But it will be noticed that on the chart the feet of the image have been separated from the legs of iron. The reason for that is this: during the present age, while it is true that the Gentile times are still running on, prophecy has to do not with this age but with the period that closed at the Cross, and another brief season that will commence after the church has been caught up to be with the Lord. God's special work in this day of grace is the taking out from among the Gentiles a people to the name of His Son. He is not now dealing with nations as such, but with individual souls, whom He is saving and, by the baptism of the Holy Spirit, forming into one body to be the bride of the Lamb in the ages to come.

Daniel shows that the times of the Gentiles began with Nebuchadnezzar. He is declared to be the head of gold of this "man of the earth" (Ps. 10:18). It is not that he alone is the fulfillment of this picture, but he represents the Babylonian Empire, which began with him and was to close with the downfall of Belshazzar, his grandson.

"After thee," says Daniel, "shall arise another kingdom inferior to thee, and another third kingdom of brass, which shall bear rule over all the earth" (v. 39). We do not need to go outside of Scripture to find out the names of these empires. In 5:31 we read, "Darius the Median took the kingdom." From the book of Esther we learn that the Persian rulers bore rule over all the earth. Darius is generally supposed to be Cyaxares II, the last king of Media; or, as some think, Gobryas, the general who led the assault on Babylon under instructions from Cyaxares and Cyrus the Persian, who united Media and Persia in one great empire. Daniel elsewhere shows us that this Medo-Persian dominion, after existing for several hundred years, would be overthrown by a mighty Grecian warrior. This was fulfilled, as we know, by Alexander the Great.

A fourth kingdom was to follow, which should be strong as iron, "forasmuch as iron breaketh in pieces and subdueth all things: and as iron that breaketh all these, shall it break in pieces and bruise" (v. 40). This can be no other than that great world power that was in existence at the birth of the Lord Jesus, when "there went out a decree from Caesar Augustus, that all the world should be taxed" (Luke 2:1). Under this empire our Lord was crucified. After His death, it continued to exist for something like five hundred years, though eventually divided into two parts, the Eastern and Western empires. Of this division the two legs may be meant to speak, though one could hardly insist on this as strongly as some do, because, from the beginning, Rome is represented by the legs of iron.

We do not have to go to history, therefore, to find out what these four great empires are. We find them all brought before us in Scripture, just in the order in which they were revealed to the king of Babylon. All this is confirmed by history, as every student knows, and is thus a remarkable proof of the inspiration of the Bible. At the time that Nebuchadnezzar dreamed his dream, the Persian kingdom did not exist. Persia was but a Babylonian satrapy. A Grecian empire might have seemed an utter impossibility. The Hellenic states were a lot of warring tribes and kingdoms, giving little promise of their future greatness. The city of Rome was just being founded—an insignificant little village on the banks of the

Tiber. How did Daniel portray with such accuracy the future history of all these powers if unaided by the Holy Spirit of God?

The metals of which the great image was composed deteriorate from the head to the feet, illustrating the continual decrease in the absolute power and magnificence of each kingdom. Nebuchadnezzar ruled as an unlimited despot. "Whom he would he slew, and whom he would he kept alive" (5:19). The rulers of the succeeding empires had their power more and more circumscribed, until in the last state of the Roman Empire we find iron mixed with miry clay, or brittle pottery—speaking of an attempted union between imperialism and democracy. Notice, also, that the specific gravity of the metals decreases each time, gold being the heaviest and iron the lightest, while feet of mingled iron and pottery would be lighter than all. No wonder such an image breaks in pieces the moment the Stone falls from heaven upon such feet! Gentile power may seem to be firmly settled on an immovable base; it may appear to be powerful enough to resist every effort aimed at its overthrow. But the hour is coming, and has now drawn near, when the Stone will fall from heaven, and the whole thing will collapse in a moment

This brings us to the last form of the fourth kingdom, for the Roman Empire, though at the present in abeyance, has not yet come to its end. The ten toes on the feet of the image represent (as a comparison with the ten horns on the Beast in chapter 7 will make plain) ten kings who are to reign at one time, but who will form a confederacy on the ground of the ancient empire. This is something which the world has never yet seen.

The commentators generally tell us that the ten-toed condition of the empire was reached in the fifth and sixth centuries, when the barbarians from the North overran the Roman Empire, and it was divided into something like ten different kingdoms. A number of different lists have been made of ten kingdoms each, but few writers agree as to the actual divisions. One thing they all seem to have overlooked: the ten kingdoms are to exist *at one time,* not through a period of several centuries, and all are to form one confederation. There is nothing in the past history of the kingdoms of Europe that answers to this. They were generally warring enemies, each seeking the destruction of others. We reject utterly this interpretation, therefore, of the ten toes. What event in the centuries of Rome's decline and fall could possibly answer to the Stone falling from heaven and the institution of the kingdom of God? And how could it be said that all the dominions represented by the image have been ground to powder when we see most of them still in existence in some form or other?

Some tell us that the Stone fell from heaven when the Lord Jesus was born into this world, and that His kingdom has been in existence and spreading through the world ever since. But Daniel says, "In the days of these kings shall the God of heaven set up a kingdom" (v. 44). That is, in the days of the ten kings, that kingdom is to be established. Now the ten-kingdomed condition of the empire had certainly not been reached at the Incarnation. Rome remained an undivided kingdom for three hundred years after the birth of Christ, and for two hundred years more it existed as the Eastern and Western empires. Manifestly, then, the birth into this world of the Son of God is not the event here prophesied. Gentile dominion was not overturned and destroyed at that time, nor since; therefore, we look on to the future for it.

To attempt to locate the falling of the Stone in the fifth or sixth century is the height of absurdity. In what sense did the God of heaven then set up a kingdom? That was the very time when the bishop of Rome was struggling for supremacy over the church and the nations. It was followed by a thousand years of darkness, when the Word of God was lost to the masses, superstition took the place of faith, iniquity ruled in high places—both civil and ecclesiastical—and peace seemed to be taken from the earth. Surely all this is very different indeed from Christ's predicted reign of righteousness and blessing. Manifestly then the Stone has not fallen from heaven, though how soon it will do so no mortal can say.

I desire to trace out a little of what Scripture has to tell us elsewhere about this Stone. It is undoubtedly a figure of the Lord Jesus Christ. Psalm 118:22 tells us, long before He came into this scene, that He would be the Stone set at naught by the builders and become the head of the corner. In the New Testament this verse is declared to be prophetic of Christ. When He came to earth He was indeed the Stone set at naught by the builders, the rulers of the Jews, but mark, He did not come as the Stone falling from heaven. That is the way He will come when He returns the second time. "He came [before] unto his own, but his own received him not" (John 1:11). He came here as the Foundation Stone, the Head Stone of the corner. But they who should have owned His claims, cried in their unbelief and hatred, "Away with Him; crucify Him; crucify Him!" Now God has taken Him up to heaven. Yonder, in the Father's glory, the eye of faith beholds that exalted Stone. The day is coming when it is going to fall upon His enemies, and when it falls, it will grind to powder all Gentile dominion and all those who have rejected the precious grace of God.

In Isaiah 8:14 Christ is prophetically described as a Stone of stumbling and a Rock of offense. We are told that many will stumble and fall. Thus it was when He came in lowly grace: "They stumbled at the stumbling Stone, as it is written." They were looking for a great world monarch. When He came in humiliation,

Israel nationally stumbled over Him, and they were broken—and they remain broken to this day. Whenever you see a Jew walking the streets of a Gentile city, you may say in your heart, There is a proof of the truth of what the Lord Jesus has said, "Whosoever shall fall on this stone shall be broken" (Matt. 21:44; Luke 20:18). Broken, and scattered, and peeled, they have wandered in all the lands of the earth, hardly welcome anywhere, until, in these last days, God has been turning the hearts of the nations toward them, preparatory to their being taken back to their own land. By and by a remnant will return to the Lord, so Isaiah 28:16 says, "Behold, I lay in Zion for a foundation a stone, a tried stone, a precious corner stone, a sure foundation: he that believeth shall not make haste." He then goes on depicting Israel's deliverance at the second appearing of this Stone of salvation. He it is who is described in Zechariah 3:9 as the Stone engraved with the engraving of a signet, upon which shall be seven eyes.

But what about the nations in that day? The message of grace has gone out to them. What has been the result? God has been taking out from among them a people for His name, but the mass have deliberately rejected the Christ of God and that rejected Lord Jesus is soon going to fall upon them in judgment. Then will the rest of His word be fulfilled, "On whomsoever it shall fall, it will grind him to powder" (Matt. 21:44; Luke 20:18). Israel stumbled over Him, and they are broken. He is going to fall upon the Gentiles in His wrath and indignation, and they will be ground to powder and driven away from before His face like the chaff of the summer threshing floor.

Do you ask, "When is the Stone going to fall?" It will be when the countries once occupied by the Roman Empire in Europe will make a ten-kingdom coalition, electing one of their number to be their supreme arbiter. We have him set forth in chapter 7 as the little horn rising out of the Roman Empire—a passage which has been often applied to the pope but which we shall see has no application to him at all. In that day the iron of imperial power will be mixed with the brittle pottery of socialism and democracy, but they will not cleave together.

We see this preparing at the present time. When, for instance, I read the account of the peace conferences, and similar conventions, I have no thought that lasting universal peace is going to be brought about in that way, while the Prince of Peace is still rejected. But I think I see the shadow on the wall of this revived Roman Empire. From my study of the Word of God, I quite expect one of two things: either universal war or universal arbitration. As a result of either of these methods, the ten-kingdomed form of the Roman Empire will be brought about.

Before that day arrives, the church will have been caught away to heaven, so no believer of the present dispensation will be upon the earth when these things are in process of fulfillment. But there may be many to whom these words shall come who will still be living on this earth in the days of the feet of the image—the last solemn period of the times of the Gentiles. Awful will it be to dwell in this scene then—to participate in the judgment when the Stone falls from heaven. If these words reach one who is still out of Christ, let me warn you faithfully that if you go on rejecting the Lord Jesus a little longer, if you continue to harden your heart, if you turn "away the shoulder" (Zech. 7:11), if you close your ears and shut your eyes to the truth of God, you may be numbered among those left behind when the Lord calls for His redeemed ones to rise to meet Him in the air. Then there will be, for you, nothing "but a certain fearful looking for of judgment and fiery indignation, which shall devour the adversaries" (Heb. 10:27). Think what it will mean to be thus left for the vengeance of God!

If you have not yet heeded the voice of Him who pleads in grace, get down on your face before Him now, I beseech you, and cry, "I am vile, and repent in dust and ashes!" Then remember that "if thou shalt confess with thy mouth the Lord Jesus, and shalt believe in thine heart that God hath raised him from the dead, thou shalt be saved. For with the heart man believeth unto righteousness; and with the mouth confession is made unto salvation" (Rom. 10:9–10). Thus shall you be ready to hail His coming with joy, whose return would otherwise mean for you the end of mercy's day, the sealing of your doom.

I would remark in closing that while Nebuchadnezzar fell upon his face, worshiped Daniel, and acknowledged that his God was a God of gods, a Lord of kings, and a revealer of secrets, yet there is no evidence that his conscience had been reached by the revelation made to him of God's wisdom and power. He advanced Daniel to a position of trust and confidence, and at his request set Shadrach, Meshach, and Abednego over the affairs of the province of Babylon. But the God of Daniel he was not yet ready to own as *his* God and the only Savior. He was still to him *a* god, albeit greater than other deities. He was soon to know Him as *the* God who alone "ruleth in the kingdom of men" (4:17).

LECTURE 3

THE ABOMINATION
OF DESOLATION IN TYPE

Daniel 3

In that which now claims our attention we shall see how little Nebuchadnezzar had profited by the revelation God had made to him. We have already noticed that when Daniel explained the meaning of the dream, Nebuchadnezzar fell down before the prophet and did him homage. He had many nice things to say to him, and he gave him great rewards. But he was not brought to repentance or humbled in self-judgment before the God who had thus manifested His omniscient power. The king could appreciate the wisdom of Daniel, but he had no heart for the God who had inspired His servant.

Nebuchadnezzar is not alone in that. Many there are who have a certain admiration for the ministry and the Word of God, but yet who themselves go on practically all through their lives strangers to Him whose Word His ministers declare. This was Nebuchadnezzar's condition exactly at this time. For in this third chapter we see that, instead of his being humbled by the revelation made, it simply served to exalt himself as one especially favored of heaven and to magnify his thoughts of the human mind and his own greatness.

29

This reminds me of another man who was favored with a remarkable revelation, of whom we read in the New Testament. I refer to the apostle Paul, who was caught up to the third heaven. And this man Paul, though a child of God and a most devoted servant of Christ in every way, had just the same kind of a heart that Nebuchadnezzar had. So, in order that he might not be lifted up because of the abundance of the revelation, there was given him a thorn in the flesh to remind him of his human weakness. Thus we are reminded that even divine truth, if not held in fellowship with God, may actually be used to puff one up. Mere knowledge, apart from divine love, puffs up. This is not the case with spiritual discernment, because the very first requisite for spirituality is humility. Spiritual discernment comes from God, and that will not exalt anyone. But even scriptural knowledge, if divorced from godliness, will have a very deleterious effect upon the mind and heart. That was the way it was with Nebuchadnezzar. But in the next chapter we shall see how he too got his thorn in the flesh and its blessed result.

What is emphasized here is that Nebuchadnezzar is lifted up with pride, and he determines to make a great image (probably a replica of the one he had seen in his dream) and call upon all men to bow to it. It was really to set forth the power and glory of *man,* for it pictured Gentile dominion in independence of God. It is stamped with the same number that distinguishes the Beast in Revelation 13—the number of a man, six hundred sixty-six. You will notice the passage tells us that it was sixty cubits high and six cubits broad. Seven is the number that speaks of spiritual completeness. Six seems to tell us of man's greatest efforts to attain to perfection.

The image was accordingly made and set up in the plain of Dura. A command then went forth that upon the sounding of a great orchestra, all the peoples, nations, and languages gathered together from all the various provinces of the empire should fall down and worship it. If any refused, they were to be cast into a furnace of fire.

The special place given to the great orchestra is very noticeable, as much so as in large worldly religious gatherings at the present time. It excites the emotions and, thus working upon the feelings, gives people a sense of devotion and religiousness, which after all may be very unreal. In the Old Testament dispensation, musical instruments were used in the ornate temple services, but there is certainly no warrant for it in the New Testament. People may call it worship to sit and listen to a trained, and possibly unconverted, choir and orchestra rendering sweet and touching strains. But the music simply acts upon the sensuous part of our natures and has nothing to do with true adoration of the Father and the Son, which must be in spirit and in truth to be acceptable to God. Those who plead for its use, because of the place it had in Old Testament times, should remember that that was a typical dispensation. The instruments then used typified the melody now made in the hearts of God's redeemed ones. We sometimes sing, and very truly—

> O Lord, we know it matters not
> How sweet the song may be;
> No heart but of the Spirit taught
> Makes melody to Thee.

A minister once remarked to me that many esthetic persons attended his church *to worship God in music,* so he sought to have the best performers and the finest music it was possible to obtain, as otherwise the people would not attend. What a delusion it all is! And yet people actually look upon that as really worshiping God, whether they have ever been converted or not! In reality they are only gratifying their own taste for melody and harmony—a taste God-given, I grant you, and proper enough in its place, but not to be confounded with true worship. A heart filled with Christ gives forth the sweetest music that ever reaches the ear of God the Father. He says, "Whoso offereth praise glorifieth me" (Ps. 50:23). Let us remember, then, that in the New Testament dispensation it is "singing and making melody in your heart to the Lord" (Eph. 5:19) to which the Christian is exhorted. That is where the music is to be—a heart full of praises to the God of all grace. May we know more of it.

I remember on one occasion taking a friend of mine—unquestionably an earnest Christian—into a little hall where perhaps half a hundred believers were gathered together one Lord's day morning for worship. He had been accustomed to a service very much like that which I have referred to above. On that particular morning it seemed to me the Lord's presence in our midst was especially manifest. One after another took part in praise and thanksgiving, as the Holy Spirit seemed to lead. Together we broke the bread and partook of the cup that speaks so loudly to the Christian heart of Him who gave Himself for us. At times there was hardly a dry eye in the room as we remembered Him who in infinite grace had redeemed us to God. Returning home, I inquired of my friend if he had enjoyed the meeting. He replied, "Oh, very well. There were many things about it that appealed to me very much. But I did miss the music." "Why," I replied, "did you not hear the music?" "Music?" was the answer, "why, there was none there." "Indeed there was," I answered. "Each heart that was occupied with Christ was like a stringed instrument touched by His own blessed hand, and He, the chief singer on the stringed instruments,[1] was there in our midst, leading out our hearts in worship and praise to the Father." But, alas, my friend did not seem able to enter into this! How is it with you, my hearer? Have you yet learned what it is to "worship . . . in spirit and in truth" (John 4:23–24)?

But, turning back to our subject, we notice that the instruments were to play. The people were to be stirred up by the music, and then they were all to prostrate themselves before the great image that set forth the glory of man.

But there were three in that great company who paid no heed to the king's commandment. Shadrach, Meshach, and Abednego refused to bow, and malignant spies soon carried the news to the haughty monarch. They said, "There are certain Jews . . . O king, have not regarded thee: they serve not thy gods, nor worship the golden image which thou hast set up" (v. 12). In a rage, the king sent for the three devoted men. He offered to give them another opportunity to carry out his bidding; otherwise they must suffer the fate reserved for any who would not worship the image. Shadrach, Meshach, and Abednego were not like the timeservers of these degenerate days; they were not like the trucklers to the present age. They knew God had said, "Thou shalt *not* make unto thee any graven image . . . thou shalt *not* bow down thyself to them, nor serve them" (Exod. 20:4–5). So these three Hebrews boldly faced the great king and said: "O Nebuchadnezzar, we are not careful to answer thee in this matter. If it be so, our God whom we serve is able to deliver us from the burning fiery furnace, and he will deliver us out of thine hand, O king. But if not, be it known unto thee, O king, that we will not serve thy gods, nor worship the golden image which thou hast set up" (vv. 16–18). Thus they witnessed a good confession, and in their God-given strength boldly stood before the king and all the people as the witnesses of Jehovah's power and glory.

In his rage and fury, Nebuchadnezzar ordered that the furnace be heated seven times more than ordinarily and that his instructions be carried out to the letter. So great was the furnace's heat that it consumed the men who cast them into the flames. Then we read that Nebuchadnezzar arose and came to the furnace and cried out in amazement, "Did not we cast three men bound into the midst of the fire? . . . Lo, I see four men loose, walking in the midst of the fire, and they have no hurt; and the form of the fourth is like [a son] of God [or son of the gods]" (vv. 24–25). We know well who that fourth One was, so that the rendering that we have in the Authorized Version is correct as to the person, whether it is actually what Nebuchadnezzar meant or not. The blessed Son of God was there with His dear servants in their hour of trial. He had said long before through the prophet Isaiah, "When thou walkest through the fire, thou shalt not be burned; neither shall the flame kindle upon thee" (Isa. 43:2). And every Word of God shall be fulfilled, "for he is faithful that promised" (Heb. 10:23).

We are not told that anyone but Nebuchadnezzar saw the form of this fourth One. He cried out at once, "Shadrach, Meshach, and Abed-nego, ye servants of the most high God, come forth, and come hither" (v. 26). And they came forth, not having the smell of fire upon them; the flame had simply burned away their bonds and left them free men. The result was that Nebuchadnezzar was filled with admiration for the power of the great God of Shadrach, Meshach, and Abednego. He made a royal decree declaring that anyone who should speak anything amiss against their God should be put to death. Yet, as before, when his dream was interpreted, he does not bow in repentance at the feet of the Lord and own Him as *his* God. He simply speaks of Him as *their* God, and while he admires His greatness and power, he does not worship and serve the Lord Jehovah.

How many people there are in the world just like that! They would not say anything against God our Father nor His Son the Lord Jesus Christ. They have a certain reverence in their hearts for God. They think of Him as their mother's God, perhaps, or the God of their fathers, but they cannot cry, "*My* Lord and *my* God" (John 20:28), as Thomas did after he saw the print of the nails. And so again we are reminded that it is one thing to give assent to the truth of Scripture and the revelation there given as to the glory of the triune God, but it is quite another to have bowed the heart in His presence, owned oneself a sinner lost and guilty, and trusted God's blessed Son, the crucified and risen Savior, as our own deliverer. Nebuchadnezzar owns His *power*, but he does not yet own His *claims* upon him. He had to pass through a humiliating experience before he would come to that.

But someone may be inquiring, What has all this to do with prophecy? Why did God cause this particular bit of history to be recorded in the book of the prophet Daniel? This would have been something very suitable in a historical book or a devotional book, but why do we have it here in a prophetic book? For a very good reason indeed. This event, though actual history, is a typical scene picturing the trial and deliverance of a faithful remnant of Daniel's people that is to take place in the time of the end. There will come a day when (like the great image set up by Nebuchadnezzar) what the Lord Jesus calls "the abomination of desolation, spoken of by Daniel the prophet" (Matt. 24:15), is going to be set up in Jerusalem by the Antichrist of the future.

After the church has been caught away to heaven at the close of this dispensation, the Jews (who are even now returning to Palestine in large numbers) will be deceived into owning the claims of a blasphemous impostor claiming to be the Messiah. He it is who is going to place "the abomination that maketh desolate" (11:31; 12:11). He will demand that all men worship the image that he sets up, and thus the scene of the plain of Dura will be reenacted. In that day, as in the past, a remnant among the Jews will refuse to own his claims or to obey his voice. This will be the signal for the breaking out of the Great Tribulation, "the time of Jacob's trouble" (Jer. 30:7). But many of the faithful shall be saved out of it, just as these three Hebrew young men were preserved by God in the midst of, and eventually delivered from, the furnace of fire.

Some may ask, What is the abomination of desolation? I cannot tell you positively. Scripture has not clearly revealed it. It seems to be identified with the image of the Beast set up by the False Prophet, as predicted in Revelation 13, and which he will cause all men to worship—all who have not the seal of God. This image of the Beast may not be a literal idol. It may be that it refers to some great popular movement. But it seems to be intimately connected with that of which our Lord warned His disciples. At any rate, it speaks of a time when men will be called upon to acknowledge the power and the authority of that which is satanic instead of divine and when practically all the world will be brought to own the Antichrist as the Messiah.

It is a mistake to suppose that the Antichrist is the papacy. We shall see very clearly, I trust, when we come to consider the latter part of the eleventh chapter, that he will be a distinct personality—a Jew by birth, who will bear rule in the land of Palestine and be accepted by the Jews as their Messiah. He will deny the Father and the Son, and be energized and controlled by the Devil. In that day apostate Christendom will join with apostate Judaism in owning allegiance to this monster of iniquity. But, according to His promise, God will, even in that day when iniquity shall come in like a flood, lift up a standard against it. He will have His faithful little flock who will dare to stand, like Shadrach, Meshach, and Abednego, for the truth which He will have made known to them. Though because of this they become the victims of Satan's rage and man's hatred, yet they shall be delivered out of it all, to the glory of the God whom they shall serve. No weapon that is formed against them shall prosper, for the Most High shall be their shield and buckler.

Already we see preparations being made for these momentous events. While they are not to take place as long as the church remains on earth, yet even now the land of Palestine is being prepared by God to become once more the home of His earthly people, and the people are being prepared for their land. Think of the changes that have been taking place in the East in the last fifty years! A half century ago a Jew was not allowed to dwell inside the walls of the city of Jerusalem, and there were less than fifty thousand Jews in all Palestine. Now there are more than that number living in Jerusalem itself, and it is estimated that there are nearly three times that number dwelling in the land. And now, the latter rains that God had withdrawn in judgment for many centuries are returning to the land once more. While they have not come every year, yet there has been sufficient rain to encourage agriculturists to such an extent that thousands of acres have been planted as olive yards, vineyards, and fruit farms. Most of these are owned and worked by Jews. Of course all these things are very different from the fulfillment of the prophecies in regard to their regathering by omnipotent power. But they show us that things are shaping themselves for the carrying out of the predictions as to the Great Tribulation and the events that are to follow in rapid succession.

In the hour of Antichrist's dreadful reign it will mean much to be faithful to God; it will mean much *not* to own the abomination of desolation. But grace will be given to the feeble remnant, and they shall glorify God in the fires. If such is to be the triumph of saints in a future day, what devotion and faithfulness should characterize us who are so much more highly favored in this present dispensation of the grace of God! And yet how many there are who fail to stand the test when it comes to maintaining that which God has committed to them! How little the most of us know of that spirit of devotion to Christ that led Athanasius of old to reply to the emperor's taunt, "All the world is against you," by the never-to-be-forgotten words, "Then I am against all the world!"

It was this spirit that enabled Paul to triumph when he stood before Nero, even though he had to say, "At my first answer no man stood by me." Left alone, he nevertheless bore a faithful witness and "was delivered out of the mouth of the lion."

What a rebuke are these devoted servants of God to many of us today! How little do we know of standing for Christ and His truth, even if we have to stand alone! But how contemptible will our weakness and pusillanimity appear in that coming day of glory! Rest assured, there will not be a saint then who will regret having suffered for Christ or borne reproach for His name's sake, but there will be thousands who would give worlds, were they theirs to give, if they had been but more faithful and devoted while in this scene of testing.

The time is short. Our day of testimony for an absent Lord will soon be over. Oh, let us not forget that we have

> Only one life—'twill soon be past;
> Only what's done for Jesus will last.

NEBUCHADNEZZAR'S HUMBLING: GENTILE SUBJUGATION TYPIFIED

Daniel 4

In Job 33:14–17, we are told, "God speaketh once, yea, twice, yet man perceiveth it not. In a dream, in a vision of the night, when deep sleep falleth upon men, in slumberings upon the bed; then he openeth the ears of men, and sealeth their instruction, that he may withdraw man from his purpose [or work], and hide pride from man." This is how God often speaks to men where they do not have open Bibles to give them the clear revelation of His will. He has many ways of reaching those who seem bent upon their own destruction. This fourth chapter of Daniel is a remarkable example of God's matchless grace and illustrates most preciously the words of Elihu.

God had spoken *once* to Nebuchadnezzar in giving him the dream of the great image of the times of the Gentiles. But the heart of the king was willful, and he continued to go on with his own purpose in his pride and folly. God spoke *twice* by the marvelous vision of the Son of God in the midst of the fiery furnace, keeping His faithful witnesses from all danger and harm. But again the proud king kept on his way, with unsubject heart and unsubdued will. Now God speaks the *third* time, and this in a most humiliating manner, to this great world ruler's confusion before his princes.

In the passage in Job, Elihu goes on to show that when dreams and visions do not avail, God sometimes allows disease to grip the body until the poor sinner is broken in spirit and crushed in heart, ready at last to cry, "I have sinned, and perverted that which was right, and it profited me not" (Job 33:27). "*Then* he is gracious unto him, and saith, Deliver him from going down to the pit: I have found a ransom" (v. 24).

So, in this stirring chapter, written by Nebuchadnezzar himself, and preserved and incorporated into the volume of inspiration by Daniel, we have the interesting account of the means God used to bring this haughty king to the end of himself and lead him to abase himself before the Majesty in the heavens. In other words, this is Nebuchadnezzar's conversion and seems clearly to show that a work of grace took place in his soul before he laid down the scepter entrusted to his hand by Jehovah. It is typical too, no doubt. For in Nebuchadnezzar we see a picture of all Gentile power—its departure from God, its degradation and bestial character, and its final subjugation to God in the time of the end when Christ shall return in glory and all nations shall prostrate themselves before Him, owning His righteous and benevolent sway. Nebuchadnezzar set up in intelligence was the embodiment of authority given from heaven: "The powers that be are ordained of God" (Rom. 13:1). But it is written, "Man being in honour abideth not: he is like the beasts that perish" (Ps. 49:12). This the king's madness clearly sets forth—the turning away of the nations from God and the corruption of governments to serve human ends. Has not this been characteristic of the great ones of this world? Instead of kings standing for God and acting as His representatives to maintain justice and judgment in the earth, do we not find pride and self-will, covetousness and self-seeking, generally controlling them? All this is pictured by the debasement of Nebuchadnezzar when his heart was changed to the heart of a beast, and he was driven forth to eat grass like the oxen of the fields.

But the day draws near when God will assert Himself and all Gentile dominion shall come to an end. Then the long-promised King will shine forth in His glorious majesty, and the kings of the earth shall bring their glory and honor unto the New Jerusalem, the heavenly throne-city of the coming kingdom. Then will the nations look up as redeemed men and not down as the beasts that perish.

Even in this present age history teaches us the value of a national recognition of God's moral government. We have heard of the heathen chieftain who came from his distant domain to visit Queen Victoria. One day he asked her if she would tell him the secret of England's progress and greatness. For answer, it is said, the queen presented him with a Bible, saying, "This book will tell you." Who can doubt that according to the measure in which that Book of books has been believed and loved by any people, God has honored them, and you will find that every nation that has welcomed and protected the gospel has been cared for and blessed in a special way.

On the other hand, let there be a national rejection of His Word, as in the case of the French nation, who were among the first favored by Him in Reformation times but drove out the truth He gave them, and you will find disaster following disaster. For He who cannot lie has said, "Them that honour me I will honour, and they that despise me shall be lightly esteemed" (1 Sam. 2:30).

But let us now turn directly to our chapter for a concrete example of all this. It begins with, "Nebuchadnezzar the king, unto all people, nations, and languages, that dwell in all the earth" (v. 1). This comes home to my heart in a most marked way. I realize that I am reading the personal testimony of one who was in some respects the greatest monarch this world has ever known. I am privileged to have his own account of how he—a proud, self-willed man—was brought to repentance and to the saving knowledge of the God of all grace! For, as already intimated, I gather from this proclamation that this mighty potentate was quickened from on high, and that a divine work was accomplished in his soul by that ever-blessed One who, in mercy, had revealed Himself to him.

What a wonderful thing this is! And what a miracle! The fact is, every conversion is a miracle—every soul that is saved knows what it is to be dealt with in supernatural power. It is God alone who changes men about like this. He picks up a vile, wretched sinner and makes him a holy, happy saint. He works in the drunkard's soul and changes him to a sober, useful member of society. He breaks down the proud and stubborn, and they become meek and lowly, easy to be entreated. Are not these things miracles? Surely! And they are being enacted all around us. Yet men sneer and say the miraculous never happens in this law-controlled, workaday world of ours! Oh that men might have their eyes opened to *see* and their ears to *hear* what God in His grace is doing on the basis of the one offering for sin of His blessed Son upon the Cross!

"I thought it good," Nebuchadnezzar goes on, "to show the signs and wonders that the high God hath wrought toward me. How great are his signs! and how mighty are his wonders! his kingdom is an everlasting kingdom, and his dominion is from generation to generation" (vv. 2–3). What a splendid confession this is, and how different from his previous acknowledgments in chapters 2 and 3! Ah, his conscience has been reached now, and he knows God for himself, and delights to tell of His signs and wonders wrought toward *him!* He owns

Him now not as *a* god, but as the one true and living God whose "kingdom ruleth over all" (Ps. 103:19) and shall continue forevermore.

This is not, of course, the mediatorial kingdom of Christ of which he speaks, but God's moral government of the universe, which nothing ever alters for a moment.

And now I would like to be very personal and press some questions home upon each listener. Have *you* anything to tell about the signs and wonders that the high God has wrought toward you? Have you ever been brought into direct contact with Him, so that you can speak confidently of what He has done for your soul? Have you been humbled by getting a sight of yourself as a lost, undone sinner before Him? Have you taken that place—your only rightful place—and owned yourself unclean and undone, in dire need of sovereign mercy? And do you know what it is to have fled for refuge to the very God against whom you have sinned so grievously and to have found in His Son our Lord Jesus Christ a hiding place from the judgment your sins deserved? I beseech you, do not attempt to turn these questions to one side. But if you cannot answer each one unhesitatingly in the affirmative, stop and ponder them again. Ask yourself if there is any valid reason why you should longer persist in your neglect of God's way of salvation, and why you should longer leave your soul in jeopardy. Oh that Nebuchadnezzar's testimony might speak loudly to your heart and conscience if you are still a stranger to the God he had learned to adore.

Something very definite had been done for his soul, and he delighted to tell of it and to give an answer to every man as to the reason of the hope that was in him.

Before God awakened him, he had been "at rest in [his] house, and flourishing in [his] palace" (v. 4). Think of that! At rest and flourishing while still in his sins and a stranger to God! Ah, there is a deceitful rest, a deceitful peace, which lulls many a soul into a false security. To be untroubled is no evidence of safety. To be at peace does not prove that all is well. I once caught hold of a blind man and drew him back just in time to keep him from plunging headlong into an open cellar way. He thought all was well and was in peace of mind as he walked along. Yet, two more steps, and he would have gone down! Be sure that your peace is one founded on the blood of Christ shed upon the Cross, and you will then have that peace which is true and lasting. Every other is false and fleeting. The peace of God is that which comes from relying on the testimony of God and follows exercise as to the sins that have separated the soul from Him.

Nebuchadnezzar tells us how he was aroused from that false security in which he had dwelt for so long. "I saw a dream," he says, "which made me afraid, and the thoughts upon my bed and the visions of my head troubled me" (v. 5). The

vision was sent for this very purpose. God saw that he needed to be troubled—
he needed to be awakened from his sleep of death. It was grace that thus exercised him. And in some way every soul that is saved has to pass through this
period of soul anxiety and concern. Nebuchadnezzar turned, as before, to the
wrong source for help in his time of difficulty. He calls in his magicians, astrologers, Chaldeans, and soothsayers, to whom he narrates his dream, but all to no
purpose. They who before could not recall to his mind the dream that had van-
ished cannot now interpret this one.

But at last Daniel comes in, and to him the king turns expectantly. He tells
how he had seen a great tree in the midst of the earth that grew so strong and tall
that the height reached the heavens and the sight of it to the ends of the earth.
Clothed with leaves and loaded with fruit, it supplied food for all. "The beasts of
the field had shadow under it, and the fowls of the heaven dwelt in the boughs
thereof, and all flesh was fed of it" (v 12). But the king had seen a watcher and a
holy one come down from heaven, who cried aloud, saying,

> Hew down the tree, and cut off his branches, shake off his leaves, and
> scatter his fruit: let the beasts get away from under it, and the fowls
> from his branches: nevertheless leave the stump of his roots in the earth,
> even with a band of iron and brass, in the tender grass of the field; and
> let it be wet with the dew of heaven, and let his portion be with the
> beasts in the grass of the earth: let his heart be changed from man's, and
> let a beast's heart be given unto him; and let seven times pass over him.
> This matter is by the decree of the watchers, and the demand by the
> word of the holy ones: to the intent that the living may know that the
> most High ruleth in the kingdom of men, and giveth it to whomsoever
> he will, and setteth up over it the basest of men. (vv. 14–17)

This was the dream, and the king anxiously inquires if Daniel, or Belteshazzar,
could declare the interpretation of it.

The meaning was evidently clear to Daniel from the first. But we are told that
he was astonished for one hour and his thoughts troubled him. It is plain that
Nebuchadnezzar's character had in it much that was noble and admirable, and
this appealed to the prophet. He had also been highly favored by the king, and
the thought of the solemn judgment that was soon to fall upon his royal master
saddened him. Nebuchadnezzar must have discerned the anxiety and sorrow in
the face of his minister, for he speaks in a way to give him confidence to proceed
with the interpretation. It was not smooth words made up for the occasion that

were wanted. Little as he realizes what is coming, he yet desires to know the truth. It is a blessed thing for any soul to get to the place where he can say, "Give me God's Word, and let me know it *is* His word, and I will receive it, no matter how it cuts and interferes with my most cherished thoughts."

"My lord," answers Daniel, "the dream be to them that hate thee, and the interpretation thereof to thine enemies." He then goes on to explain that the great tree represented Nebuchadnezzar himself, who had been set by God in a special place of prominence in the earth as the head of all peoples and dominions. The cutting down of the tree signified that he was to be humbled to the very lowest depths, even to being driven from among men. His dwelling was to be with the beasts of the field, where he would eat grass as oxen and be wet with the dew of heaven, until seven times had passed over him, until he should know that the Most High rules in the kingdom of men and gives it unto whomsoever He will. But the fact that the stump of the tree was left indicated that his kingdom should be sure unto him after he had known that the heavens ruled. The prophet adds a word of faithful counsel, beseeching the king to break off his sins by righteousness, and his iniquities by showing mercy to the poor, in the hope that thereby the days of his tranquility might be lengthened. Observe that it is no question of earning eternal salvation of which Daniel here speaks. His advice has to do with the government of God upon earth and Nebuchadnezzar's acknowledgment and subjection to it.

All happened exactly as Daniel had said. For Nebuchadnezzar, still unhumbled though he had listened so respectfully to the words of the prophet, walked one day, a year later, in the palace of his kingdom, which was evidently upon an eminence overlooking his capital. As he walked he said to himself, "Is not this great Babylon, that I have built for the house of the kingdom by the might of my power, and for the honour of my majesty?" (v. 30). Thus did Nebuchadnezzar forget how he was indebted to the most high God for the position he occupied and the riches and the glory of it, and took all the credit to himself. While the word was in his mouth, the decree was spoken, and he was informed by a voice from heaven that the time had come when the dream should be fulfilled. The same hour he lost his reason and became a pitiable spectacle truly unfit to associate with his fellows, and he was driven from men into the open fields, where he became in very deed like the beasts that perish. We need have no difficulty in crediting this solemn account when we remember the treatment generally meted out to the insane in the oriental countries. Looked upon as the afflicted of God, they are left to wander at their own will, none interfering nor making them afraid.

Now in all this we see a picture of Gentile power in its alienation from God and bestial character. What madness have not rulers and nations been guilty of who have trampled the Word of God beneath their feet and despised His mercy and grace, refusing subjection to His government! A great tree towering up, in its independence, toward heaven is a symbol frequently used in Scripture to set forth the great ones of this world. Ezekiel uses it as a picture of the Assyrian kingdom, and in the New Testament it is used by our Lord Jesus Christ as a symbol of the kingdom of heaven as it has become in the hands of men.

"Until seven times pass over him." I want to dwell a little on that in connection with what has frequently been put forth by a certain school of prophetic teachers called "the year-day theory." This is a system of interpretation that takes prophetic seasons and times, and says all days are to be understood as years, months as thirty years, and years as periods of three hundred sixty years. Now "a time" is undoubtedly, as all are agreed, a year. Seven times, then, would be seven years. If the year-day theory be true, it would apply here as well as elsewhere in this book. But what would seven times three hundred and sixty years mean in this connection? It would amount to two thousand five hundred twenty years. In that case, Nebuchadnezzar's madness would still be going on, and he would have to eat grass as an ox for some fifty years yet. But if this be ridiculously impossible, then it is folly to attempt to apply the theory elsewhere, as this is distinctly a time prophecy.

Now in every instance where any of these time prophecies have already been fulfilled and are clearly so stated in Scripture, it is evident that days, months, or years were always fulfilled literally. For instance, God said of the antediluvians that their days should be one hundred twenty years, and in exactly that length of time the world, that then was was overthrown with a flood. Suppose the year-day theory had been held by Noah; he would have calculated that there certainly could be no hurry in building the ark, inasmuch as the Flood could not come for at least forty-three thousand two hundred years, or one hundred twenty prophetic years of three hundred sixty literal years each. Again, God told Moses that the children of Israel, because of their unbelief, should wander in the wilderness for forty years, according to the number of the days in which they had searched the land. Now here, if anywhere, we might be supposed to have authority for this year-day theory; but, on the contrary, we have the very opposite. Days mean days, and years mean years.

In the book of Ezekiel the prophet was told to lie upon his left side for three hundred and ninety days, that he might bear the iniquity of the house of Israel. Then he was to lie upon his right side forty days to bear the iniquity of the house of Judah, and God adds "I have appointed thee each day for a year" (Ezek. 4:6). This passage is often adduced as evidence of the scripturalness of the theory referred to. But surely it gives no title from which to reason that wherever times and seasons are specified in the prophetic Scriptures the principle of a day for a year can be relied upon as correct. In the case of the great prophecy of the seventy weeks, it might appear that we have a case in point. But there, as we shall see when we come to consider the ninth chapter, the term *week* does not necessarily refer to seven days at all.

The fact is that all kinds of contradictory systems have been built up on this year-day conception, and dates have been set again and again for the second coming of the Lord and the fulfillment of other prophetic events only to result in disappointment and confusion, and to give occasion to the enemies of the truth to blaspheme when the dates specified have passed away with nothing of moment occurring upon them. The whole thing rests on supposing something that God had never revealed.

In the instance before us, Daniel declared that the king would be mad until seven times had passed over him, and in exactly seven years Nebuchadnezzar lifted up his eyes. His reason returned to him. He saw that God had been dealing with him. His lesson was learned. He blessed the most high God. He turned to Him in repentance and owned Him as his God. Then he wrote out this account of his conversion that others might, with him, be humbled before the only true God and bless Him for His mercy.

Thus will it be with the spared nations after the judgments that are to take place in the time of the end. Nebuchadnezzar aptly typifies all Gentile power, as we have already noticed. It has been haughty, insolent, and heaven defying. Forgetting God, the true source of authority and power, it has become like the beasts of the earth. You know something of its course since it crucified the Lord of glory. The nations have been mad—as utterly bereft of all true reason as was the demented king of Babylon. But the day is nearing when God, in His grace, is going to end all this and deliver a groaning world from the evils of selfish despotism and national jealousies. Christ's personal return from heaven will conclude the long period of Gentile misrule. Creation groans for the hour when the one true King will be manifested, when our Lord Jesus Christ "in his times he shall show, who is the blessed and only Potentate, the King of kings, and Lord of lords" (1 Tim. 6:15).

"The blessed Potentate," that is, a truly happy ruler! The world has never seen a happy potentate in the past. Shakespeare's line has passed into a proverb, "Uneasy lies the head that wears a crown." But in the days of our Lord Jesus Christ, when

He takes the rod of power and reigns in righteousness, the world, for the first time, will see a *happy* Potentate. Who can measure the happiness of the Son of God when He descends to take the kingdom for which He has waited so long, when He has His own beloved bride with Himself to share His glory! Then He shall see of the travail of His soul and shall be satisfied. Those will be the days of heaven upon earth of which we read in the Canticles, when "the time of the singing" shall have come and all redeemed creation will rejoice beneath Immanuel's rule.

Our translators have put in two little words in that verse which do not belong there. They have made it say, "The time of the singing *of birds* is come" (Song 2:12). Oh, how they have weakened it! It should simply read, "The time of the singing is come"—the time when the heavenly saints will be hymning His praises from the glory; when Israel, blessed on the earth, will rejoice in His loving-kindness; when all creation will fall at His feet to worship, and He will joy over them with singing in that day of the gladness of His heart. Then He will show who is that happy and only Potentate.

"That happy Potentate" excludes all sorrow and disappointment. "That only Potentate" excludes every other ruler. Upon His head will be many crowns. Every other crown will be cast at His feet, and He will reign as King of kings and Lord of lords. Happy for those, in that day, who have humbled themselves in this, and who, like Nebuchadnezzar, have owned the righteousness of His dealings with them; who have confessed their sins before Him; and who will be able to exclaim with joy when He descends in majesty, "This is our God; we have waited for him" (Isa. 25:9). Of such He will cry with rejoicing, "Gather my saints together unto me; those that have made a covenant with me by sacrifice" (Ps. 50:5).

Before that day dawns, it is the path of wisdom to "kiss the Son, lest he be angry, and ye perish from the way, when his wrath is kindled but a little" (Ps. 2:12). Have *you* kissed the Son? I mean, have you bowed in contrition at the feet of the Lord Jesus Christ and trusted Him as your own Savior and owned Him as your rightful Lord? If you have, you can look up and say with happy confidence, "Come, Lord Jesus" (Rev. 22:20). But whether you have or not, the Lord Jesus is coming—coming very soon. *Un*happy indeed will be your state for all eternity if He find you in your sins, a stranger to God and to grace. "Because there is wrath, beware lest he take thee away with his stroke: then a great ransom cannot deliver thee" (Job. 36:18). *Now,* that ransom avails for all who believe in Him. In that day the precious blood of Christ will not be offered for salvation to those who have done despite to the Spirit of grace and finally refused to heed the gospel message.

Oh, do not let the word depart,
   And close thine eyes against the light;
Poor sinner, harden not thy heart;
   Thou would'st be saved—why not tonight?

The world has nothing left to give—
   It has no true, no pure delight;
Look now to Jesus Christ, and live;
   Thou would'st be saved—why not tonight?

Our blessed Lord refuses none
   Who would to Him their souls unite;
Then be the work of grace begun;
   Thou would'st be saved—why not tonight?

BELSHAZZAR'S IMPIOUS FEAST AND OVERTHROW OF BABYLON: THE WORLD SYSTEM IN TYPE

Daniel 5

We are now to be occupied with the closing up of the history of the Babylonian Empire—the last solemn scenes in connection with the downfall of the head of gold. We shall find in it, as in the previous two chapters, a typical picture, in this instance setting forth the overthrow of Gentile power, especially in its religious character as Babylon the Great, in the time of the end. The account given of the fall of mystical Babylon in Revelation 17–18 is evidently based upon, and intimately connected with, what we have here.

And first, it is proper to remark that while the account given by Daniel of the destruction of the proud capital on the Euphrates tallies in large measure with what has been left on record by Herodotus, the so-called "Father of History," and by other ancient writers, yet the Scripture record is nevertheless challenged by a certain class of modern critics as unreliable because of alleged discrepancies between the biblical account and the inscriptions on some of the lately deciphered monuments. The chief points in question are the title given to Belshazzar, son of Nabonidus, and the identity of Darius the Median. But Belshazzar was reigning jointly with his father at this time and certainly was "king of Babylon," or "king of the Chaldeans," in the sense of being prince-regent with his seat in the imperial city. The title "king" was not applied solely to the supreme monarch in that age, nor is it necessarily so used now. It will be noticed that in chapter 2 when Daniel was honored by Nebuchadnezzar, the great king made him *second* ruler in the kingdom. But in this chapter Belshazzar appoints him to the position of *third* ruler, as he himself was clearly the second. So there is no discrepancy here, but rather that exactness which is ever found in Holy Scripture.

As to Darius the Median, his name certainly does not appear in the monuments, and Herodotus tells us that Cyrus was in command of the armies that conquered Babylon. But the name Darius need present no real difficulty as ancient kings are often known by a number of different names. In fact, no two lists of the later Median kings, as given by the old historians, agree with each other, and the monuments seem to differ from them all. The last king of the Medians was Cyaxares II, who formed an alliance with Cyrus his nephew and led a part of the armies of the confederate kingdoms to battle. His age, as given by Herodotus, agrees with that of Darius, as given in this chapter. The two may therefore be identical. On the other hand, some suppose Darius to be the same as Gobryas, who, according to ancient records, conducted the siege of Babylon as representative of the allied kings. The discrepancy in names is no greater than that in the case of Cambyses and Atrodates, both names being applied to the same monarch, the one by Xenophon, the other by Nicolas of Damascus, while it is a well-known fact that the lists of Median kings given by Ctesias and Herodotus differ in every instance, and the chronologies are hopelessly confusing and contradictory.

Yet the rationalist eagerly seizes upon any apparent discrepancy between the records left by untrustworthy and often positively dishonest chroniclers and the account given in the Word of God. The Christian need not fear that history will ever disprove what we have recorded in our Bibles. In this case, Daniel was an eyewitness. He wrote the facts as he saw and knew them. His testimony, apart from the question of divine inspiration, is surely more to be relied upon than that of fawning courtiers or hearsay historians whose professed facts are often untrustworthy, highly colored, and opposed to each other.

What especially comes before us in this chapter is the impiety of Gentile power as represented in this rule of Belshazzar—rising to its full height in the desecration of the vessels that had been carried away from the temple of Jehovah at Jerusalem. God had committed government to the nations, giving the supreme dominion to Nebuchadnezzar. But we find that from the beginning they failed to render to

Him the honor and allegiance that were His due. Though Nebuchadnezzar himself was humbled later, his successors—Evil-Merodach,[1] Nabonidus, and his impious son—fail utterly to profit by the lesson their illustrious ancestor had learned at so great a cost to himself.

In all this it is easy to see pictured the whole course of government as entrusted to man. Proud, haughty rulers delight to make capital out of the fact that "the powers that be are ordained of God" (Rom. 13:1). But it is generally with no thought of seeking His glory or of acting as His representatives upon the earth, but rather to establish and augment their own power by deducing therefrom the doctrine of "the divine right of kings."

A little before our chapter opens, Cyrus the Great, king of Persia, had entered into an alliance with Cyaxares II, his aged uncle, and the combined kingdoms had subdued various nations to the north and south. They now determined to annex the fast-decaying Babylonian Empire to their dominions. In this, Cyrus was evidently the leading spirit, though while Cyaxares lived he was given precedence. Cyrus, though knowing it not, was "the scourge of the Lord," as Nebuchadnezzar had been before him. When Israel offended, God used the Chaldeans as His rod of chastening upon them. Now God would use the Medo-Persians for the punishment of the Chaldeans, who had shown themselves insensible to all His mercies to them.

Babylon was at this time the most magnificent and luxurious city in the world—devoted to every vice and the center and mother of idolatry. From the days of Nimrod and the Tower of Babel, until it was blotted out from under heaven, Babylon was the headquarters for the heathen mysteries. Its walls, supposedly impregnable, were so broad that several chariots could drive abreast upon them. The Euphrates ran right through the city, passing under the walls, and, of course, upon that river the people depended for their support. Yet it was destined to become their enemy, for after an unsuccessful siege of many months, the Medo-Persian armies concluded that the only way to force an entrance would be through the riverbed. Accordingly, a new channel was dug around the city without the Babylonians being aware of it. This channel connected with a nearby lake.

On that very night, when the work of turning the waters of the river out of their course would be finished and the final assault be made, Belshazzar, utterly unconscious of the danger in which the city stood, was keeping an impious feast with a thousand of his lords in honor of the heathen deities. It was not merely a feast that manifested the pride of his heart; it bore a far worse character than this, for, in insult to Jehovah, Belshazzar orders the golden vessels of the temple in Jerusalem, which had been carried down to Babylon, to be brought for use in their heathen, impious feast. Thus they drank and praised the gods of silver and gold, of brass and of stone, and forgot altogether, or blasphemed utterly, the God of heaven. On this crowning act of impiety, their cup of iniquity being full, God's sudden and sore judgment falls. God never strikes when He is dealing with nations in judgment until that moment. He could not allow the people of Israel to take possession of the land of Canaan before the days of Moses because "the iniquity of the Amorites [was] not yet full" (Gen. 15:16). And so in Babylon's case, He lingered long and permitted His people to be slaves to Nebuchadnezzar, his son, and his son's son, as foretold by Jeremiah, until the wickedness of the Chaldeans had reached its height.

At last the fateful moment had struck. At the very time that Belshazzar stood before his lords with one of the cups from Jerusalem's destroyed temple in his hand, praising his own vile demon gods, there came forth, in the full sight of all that multitude, the fingers of a man's hand, which wrote in letters of fire upon the plaster the words of doom, "MENE, MENE, TEKEL, UPHARSIN." Doubtless every noble present could decipher the strange words, but none could give their meaning or connection. When it says they could not read the words, it means they could not read them understandingly. God had written them in their own language, but who could make sense of four apparently unrelated terms: "numbered, numbered, weighed, dividing"? All instinctively recognized them as a message from the other world, but who could interpret the decree?

I think I see Belshazzar as he stands there with the wine cup in his hand. I think I see the awful look of terror that comes over his countenance—the deadly pallor that overspreads his face. I see the cup fall from his nerveless hand. I note the way in which he clings to the pillar to support his trembling limbs. The Word of God says, "His knees smote one against another" (v. 6). He called in vain, with hollow voice, for the astrologers, the soothsayers, and those learned in Chaldean lore to explain this dreadful portent. "But they could not read the writing, nor make known to the king the interpretation thereof" (v. 8). While they were in fearful consternation, the queen mother came in. She seems to have occupied a place apart from all the wickedness and revelry of that great company. Almost like the representative of another world, she appears to inform the king of one who can, she is certain, read the writing and give the interpretation of it. She says,

> There is a man in thy kingdom, in whom is the spirit of the holy gods; and in the days of thy father light and understanding and wisdom, like the wisdom of the gods, was found in him; whom the king Nebuchadnezzar thy father, the king, I say, thy father, made master of the magicians,

astrologers, Chaldeans, and soothsayers; forasmuch as an excellent spirit, and knowledge, and understanding, interpreting of dreams, and showing of hard sentences, and dissolving of doubts, were found in the same Daniel, whom the king named Belteshazzar: now let Daniel be called, and he will show the interpretation. (vv. 11–12)

Belshazzar had been utterly indifferent to the man whom God had used in the days of his grandfather Nebuchadnezzar. But Daniel had gone on in a quiet, humble way, seeking the approbation of the One who is higher than the highest. Sent for in haste, he came in to rebuke by his very presence that godless multitude. Belshazzar addressed him in flattering terms and promised him great honors if he would read the writing and show the interpretation of the thing. He should be clothed in scarlet, have a chain of gold about his neck, and be the third ruler in the kingdom.

Poor, misguided monarch! Of how little value would all his honors be on the morrow! How little would it mean to hold a fief from him as third ruler in the kingdom when the sun should rise the next day! Belshazzar little knew that while these momentous events were taking place in the palace, the waters of the river had been turned aside into the new channel, and the armies of the allied kings, a mighty horde, were coming in underneath the walls in the dry riverbed, unnoticed and undetected, because the very watchmen of the city, Herodotus tells us, were all drunk. In the streets, as in the palace, myriads of revelers were spending the night in godless amusement. Unclean orgies were being perpetrated in honor of the pagan gods, and the Persian army was upon them before they were aware of their danger.

And Daniel, I suppose, knew nothing of this either, but it makes his words to Belshazzar all the more solemn and serious.

Then Daniel answered and said before the king, Let thy gifts be to thyself, and give thy rewards to another; yet I will read the writing unto the king, and make known to him the interpretation. O thou king, the most high God gave Nebuchadnezzar thy father a kingdom, and majesty, and glory, and honour: and for the majesty that he gave him, all people, nations, and languages, trembled and feared before him: whom he would he slew; and whom he would he kept alive; and whom he would he set up; and whom he would he put down. But when his heart was lifted up, and his mind hardened in pride, he was deposed from his kingly throne, and they took his glory from him: and he was driven from the sons of men; and his heart was made like the beasts, and his dwelling was with the wild asses: they fed him with grass like oxen, and his body was wet with the dew of heaven; till he knew that the most high God ruled in the kingdom of men, and that he appointeth over it whomsoever he will. (vv. 17–21)

And now note the fearful indictment of the wretched monarch before whom he stood.

And thou his son, O Belshazzar, hast not humbled thine heart, *though thou knewest all this;* but hast lifted up thyself against the Lord of heaven; and they have brought the vessels of his house before thee, and thou, and thy lords, thy wives, and thy concubines, have drunk wine in them; and thou hast praised the gods of silver, and gold, of brass, iron, wood, and stone, which see not, nor hear, nor know: and the God in whose hand thy breath is, and whose are all thy ways, hast thou not glorified: then was the part of the hand sent from him; and this writing was written. (vv. 22–24)

Daniel did not speak to Belshazzar as he had before spoken to Nebuchadnezzar. He could not have the same respect for him that he entertained for his grandfather. You will remember when Nebuchadnezzar told his dream of the great tree that Daniel grieved to think of the suffering that he had to pass through, and said, "The dream be to them that hate thee, and the interpretation thereof to thine enemies" (v. 19). Tenderly and affectionately he besought him to repent of his evil ways. But he did not talk like that to Belshazzar. He knew *his* doom was sealed, *his* day of mercy had gone by. He saw in him only a wretched, impious degenerate who had sinned against light and knowledge, and deserved neither sympathy nor compassion. He realized that Belshazzar had gone steadily on in defiance of the God of heaven until the hour of his judgment had struck. Nothing now could avert the richly deserved wrath of the Holy One. Faithfully the prophet proceeded to press home upon the guilty king his sinfulness and impiety, and then he solemnly went on to read and interpret the message sent from heaven. Even while he was speaking, the invading hosts were drawing nearer and nearer to the palace gates, but the guilty king and his lords surrounding him were altogether unaware of what had taken place down by the river.

The meaning of the words is thus explained: *mene,* "numbered"—"God hath numbered thy kingdom, and finished it" (v. 26). Belshazzar's days of probation

were passed and gone. The day of his sentence had come. *Tekel*, "weighed"—
"Thou art weighed in the balances, and art found wanting" (v. 27). He who had
exalted himself in his pride and folly was found to be "altogether lighter than
vanity" (Ps. 62:9).

And then, note, Daniel says *peres*, "divided," a form of the same word *upharsin*
which he read from the wall, but implying that the division had already taken
place. For instead of saying, "God is dividing thy kingdom," he declares, "Thy
kingdom *is* divided, and given to the Medes and Persians" (v. 28). It was as much
as to say the blow had already fallen. It was not that God was about to do this,
but it had already been accomplished. While Daniel was interpreting, the kingdom had passed to other hands.

But the foolish and unrepentant king, despite all this, seems to fancy he is still
secure. He offers Daniel the worthless honors he had promised, attempting to
carry out the pledges made to him as though still in the zenith of his glory. But
the awful chronicle of the Holy Spirit is, "In that night was Belshazzar the king
of the Chaldeans slain. And Darius the Median took the kingdom, being about
threescore and two years old" (vv. 30–31). Thus had the history of the head of
gold come to a close, and the silver breast and arms had come upon the scene.
God's Word had been fulfilled, and that night Babylon fell to rise no more forever. In that destruction, as already intimated, we may see prefigured the overthrow of all Gentile power and dominion in the time of the end, and especially
of that evil system designated in the book of the Revelation: "BABYLON THE
GREAT, THE MOTHER OF HARLOTS AND ABOMINATIONS OF THE EARTH"
(17:5). This is the world religious system that will be destroyed just prior to the
return of the Lord from heaven.

There are those who teach that some time in the future literal Babylon is going
to be restored to be again destroyed, but a careful reading of Jeremiah 50–51 will
make it very clear, I think, to any spiritual mind that her destruction is to be
perpetual. The city is never to be revived. The Most High has visited His judgment upon it. But mystical Babylon will have reached its climax after the church
has been caught away to be with the Lord, when the papacy and all her daughters will form one great apostate organization—the refuge of all the various portions of Bible-rejecting Christendom. In *this* Babylon we see that of which the
Babylon of history was a picture.

Ancient Babylon, as we have seen, was the city of idolatry and the expression
of the pride of man's heart, combining religion with self-seeking. Idolatry, properly speaking, began there. That was the place where the great tower was made,
where men said, "Let us make us a name" (Gen. 11:4). It was no thought of

building a tower to escape another possible flood that filled their minds. But they wished a center around which to rally that they might make themselves a great name upon the earth. God had told them to scatter abroad, but they were determined not to obey Him. Unsubject in will, they turned from Him to the worship of demons. That was the beginning of heathenism. There they commenced to worship and serve the creature more than the Creator, and every idolatrous system in the world is simply an off-shoot of that first parent stem.

And so we find in the mystic Babylon of the last days the union of all human churches, only to be superseded by the worship of the Antichrist. It speaks of a glory yet to be enjoyed by the professing church after the body of Christ has been caught away to heaven, for a brief season, upon the formation of the ten-kingdomed empire, before the kings and nations of the earth sicken of the contemptible sham, and, becoming utterly atheist, burn the harlot's flesh with fire, destroying forever the great world church, who says in her heart, "I sit a queen, and am no widow, and shall see no sorrow" (Rev. 18:7).

Some may be asking, "Do you not think that Babylon the Great is already in existence?" Surely. Babylon's description in Revelation 17 coincides too exactly with history's record of the papal church to warrant any denial of her identity. What other church has sat upon the seven hills of that great city which rules over the kings of the earth? What other church has been for long centuries "drunk with the blood of the martyrs of Jesus"? What other church possessed the power and wealth ascribed to her? And where else shall we find a religious organization so delighting in names of blasphemy as she?

But the Roman communion does not alone constitute great Babylon. The harlot has daughters who, like herself, profess to be pledged to a heavenly Bridegroom while committing fornication with the world that rejected Him. "Ye adulterers and adulteresses, know ye not that the friendship of the world is enmity with God?" (James 4:4). Spiritual fornication is, at large, the union of the church and the state; individually, of the Christian with the world—an unhallowed alliance, opposed to the whole teaching of the New Testament. So if Rome be emphatically the great harlot, the state churches are her offspring—"as is the mother, so [are] her daughter[s]" (Ezek. 16:44).

Soon the daughters will be wending their way homeward, back to the arms of their evil mother. We hear much in our times of "the reunion of Christendom," and we need not think of it as the dream of impractical religious enthusiasts. Christendom will be reunited undoubtedly. Everything points to such an issue, and no serious student of the prophetic Scriptures can question it for a moment. But when it comes to pass, it will be a Christless reunion, for it will not take place until the body of Christ has been translated, and all who are left will have thrown off allegiance to the Word and Spirit of God and to the Lord Jesus Christ. The apostasy must take place first. Then the man of sin will be revealed.

Christendom's sin is the rejection of the Holy Spirit, and with that necessarily comes the rejection of the Scriptures given by the Spirit's moving upon the hearts and minds of "holy men of God." But coupled with this comes the desire for recognition as a power in the world, lording it over men's consciences. So, when the true church is caught away, all the professing systems will doubtless come together in one, and proudly exclaim, "Is not this great Babylon that we have built?" They will rejoice in a united Christendom—united in rejecting Christ, doing despite to the Holy Spirit, and throwing dishonor upon the Word of God! All will be on a carnal and satanic basis and will last but for a brief season before being overthrown with indignation by the nations, who will resent any religious obligations when the Spirit of life has departed.

This is where we see everything drifting. Babylon's pride and *hauteur* will become so insufferable that men will say, as in France, Spain, and other Latin dominions lately, "We do not want any church at all. We will destroy the whole thing and get along without it." This is the openly advocated doctrine of many Socialists and is clearly what that vaunted system of economics is leading up to, little as so-called Christian Socialists may realize it.

God will "put [it into] their hearts to fulfil his will" (Rev. 17:17). He can use one evil thing to destroy another, as He has often done in the past. He used Persia to destroy Babylon, and yet the Persians were a sinful nation, too, in due time to be overthrown by another power. And so, in the time of the end, a godless government will be used to destroy a Christless church, "for strong is the Lord God who judgeth her" (Rev. 18:8). Her doom will be as sudden and as overwhelming as was that which fell on the Babylon of Belshazzar.

> Thus with violence shall that great city Babylon be thrown down, and shall be found no more at all. And the voice of harpers, and musicians, and of pipers, and trumpeters, shall be heard no more at all in thee; and no craftsmen, of whatsoever craft he be, shall be found any more in thee; and the sound of a millstone shall be heard no more at all in thee; and the light of a candle shall shine no more at all in thee; and the voice of the bridegroom and of the bride shall be heard no more at all in thee: for thy merchants were the great men of the earth; for by thy sorceries were all nations deceived. And in her was found the blood of prophets, and of saints, and of all that were slain upon the earth. (Revelation 18:21–24)

Before that hour of the vengeance of God has been reached, the message goes forth, "Come out of her, my people, that ye be not partakers of her sins, and that ye receive not of her plagues" (Rev. 18:4). He who would be faithful to the Lord is called upon to walk apart from all that bears the impress of Babylon, remembering the word, "Have no fellowship with the unfruitful works of darkness, but rather reprove them" (Eph. 5:11). In the first chapter of Genesis we read of God creating a division, dividing the light from the darkness. This division He would ever have maintained. The Devil has been busy ever since, seeking to mix up the light and the darkness. The man of God is called to walk apart from the darkness as a child of light and of the day. May it be so with us, for His name's sake!

And now, before closing this solemn subject, I would address a word of warning to the unsaved. Belshazzar's great offense was this: though he knew of God's dealings with Nebuchadnezzar, he sinned right on, going against light and knowledge. None are so guilty as those who so act. And to all such the word comes with awful force, "He, that being often reproved hardeneth his neck, shall suddenly be destroyed, and that without remedy" (Prov. 29:1). Oh, be warned, I beseech you, if you have been for years familiar with these things. Do not longer dare to defy God to His face by casting His Word behind your back.

You little know how near you may be to the end of God's patience with you. He lingers in grace, but He may soon strike in judgment. Your *mene* may very soon be written on the wall—your days *numbered*—your life *finished! Tekel,* for you, may even now be true—*weighed,* and found wanting!

> Weighed in the balance, and wanting,—
> Weighed, but no Saviour is there,—
> Weighed, but thy soul has been trifling,—
> Weighed, and found lighter than air.

And then *peres* shall seal your doom, and your opportunities of mercy be forever gone, your body a corpse and your soul in hell! Divided—separated from all that is good, from all that is holy—to be lost forever, shut up to a Christless eternity.

O heed now the word of warning, I entreat you, and flee for your life to the city of refuge, which is Christ Jesus Himself, who says, "Him that cometh to me I will in no wise cast out" (John 6:37).

THE PRESERVATION OF THE FAITHFUL REMNANT IN TYPE

Daniel 6

In the interesting historical incident now brought before us by the pen of inspiration, we have portrayed what should be for the comfort of every trusting soul: God's tender care over all who walk uprightly before Him and confide in His love and power. Like the previous events, it also has a typical character, setting forth the peculiarly trying position in which the faithful remnant of Judah will find themselves in the days of the Antichrist.

Darius, the satrap of Babylon, was pleased, we are told, to set over the kingdom a hundred and twenty princes, and over these, three presidents, of whom Daniel was first. The prophet was thus appointed to a position very similar to that of a present-day prime minister or secretary of state. Because of the excellent spirit that was in him and his faithfulness in administering the affairs of the kingdom, he was preferred above all the other dignitaries. In this exalted office, he became, as many in similar circumstances have been, the object of the enmity and hatred of unprincipled political plotters who sought their own advancement at the expense of his downfall. Themselves corrupt, they tried to find occasion against him, taking it for granted that he was actuated by the same selfish motives as they were. But though they endeavored in every way to obtain proof of some dereliction of duty on his part, concerning which they might accuse him to the king, they at last were forced to confess, "We shall not find any occasion against this Daniel, except we find it against him concerning the law of his God" (v. 5).

The cunning plotters, knowing the intensity of his religious convictions, put their heads together, therefore, and drew up a statute, which they felt sure, if they could but prevail on the king to sign it, would ensure the downfall of his favorite. With this in mind, they came into the presence of the king and, pretending to great loyalty and zeal for the dignity of his office, said, "King Darius, live for ever. All the presidents of the kingdom, the governors, and the princes, the counsellors and the captains, have consulted together to establish a royal statute, and to make a firm decree, that whosoever shall ask a petition of any God or man, for thirty days, save of thee, O king, he shall be cast into the den of lions. Now, O king, establish the decree, and sign the writing, that it be not changed, according to the law of the Medes and Persians, which altereth not" (vv. 6–8).

Their statement was false upon the face of it, for one at least of the presidents there was, and he the chief of all, who had not been consulted in the matter. But it was he whose destruction they desired. Darius shows to poor advantage here, though in the main perhaps an excellent man, but like many another easily persuaded by the tongue of flattery. Without consulting with his chief minister, he signed the decree, thus establishing it as a law unalterable even by royal veto. By the signing of this statute, Darius practically put himself into the place that the man of sin, the lawless one, will occupy in the last days. He became a type of the Antichrist, who shall "[sit] in the temple of God, showing himself that he is God" (2 Thess. 2:4). And right here it is of moment to remark that there may be a vast difference between what a man is in himself and the place he occupies in Scripture typology. Darius, as a man, was doubtless a very different character to the coming false Messiah. He was kindly and amiable and, as we know, was afterward deeply repentant for having permitted himself to act so foolishly. But as the king, making himself an object of worship, and denying the liberty of any to offer prayers or adoration to any other God save himself, he fittingly pictures the Antichrist.

We see the same principle brought out, for instance, in the case of David, who, looked at officially, is one of the most nearly perfect types of Christ that we have in the Old Testament but who, as a man, possesses the same faults and commits as serious sins as many another.

After the vain-glorious monarch had allowed himself to be flattered into appending the seal royal to the infamous interdict, the plotters doubtless congratulated themselves that Daniel's doom was sealed. His holiness of life was a continual rebuke to their impiety, and his integrity but accentuated their crookedness. We are reminded, as we read of their inability to find anything whereof to accuse him save in the matter of the Lord his God, of that verse in the Proverbs which tells us that "when a man's ways please the LORD, he maketh even his enemies to be at peace with him [or, silent to him]" (16:7), that is, they cannot truthfully allege anything against the man who walks with God.

When Daniel knew that the writing was signed, there was on his part evidence of neither fear nor ostentation. He simply pursued his godly course, as though the decree were not in existence. Notice, verse 10 tells us, "He went into his house; and his windows *being open* in his chamber toward Jerusalem, he kneeled upon his knees three times a day, and prayed, and gave thanks before his God, *as he did aforetime."* Observe, it is not said that he opened his windows. It is quite the contrary: "His windows being open. To shut them now would be cowardice, whereas to have opened them, if he had previously been in the habit of keeping them closed, would have been to court persecution—a foolhardy thing which the child of God is never called upon to do. But Daniel remembered the words of Solomon that he prayed concerning the people of Israel:

> If they sin against thee, (for there is no man that sinneth not,) and thou be angry with them, and deliver them over before their enemies, and they carry them away captives unto a land far off or near; yet if they bethink themselves in the land whither they are carried captive, and turn and pray unto thee in the land of their captivity, saying, We have sinned, we have done amiss, and have dealt wickedly; if they return to thee with all their heart and with all their soul in the land of their captivity, whither they have carried them captives, and pray toward their land, which thou gavest unto their fathers, and toward the city which thou hast chosen, and toward the house which I have built for thy name: then hear thou from the heavens, even from thy dwellingplace, their prayer and their supplications, and maintain their cause, and forgive thy people which have sinned against thee. (2 Chronicles 6:36–39)

In full accord with this, Daniel went up into his house three times daily. Bowing down upon his knees before his windows opened toward Jerusalem, he offered his prayers and thanksgivings and made his confession to his God. And now when he knows that he takes his life in his hand each time he carries out his pious custom, he does not shrink for a moment or seek in any way to hide from his enemies the fact that he has to do with the God of Israel. As he kneels with bowed head facing the direction of the desolated city of Jehovah, Jerusalem, the place where the Lord had set His name, we may be assured that his prayer was nonetheless fervent and his thanksgiving nonetheless real, because he knew, as he could not help but know, that malignant spies were waiting to report his conduct to the king who, according to the unalterable laws of the Medes and Persians, was bound to carry out its provisions and to visit upon each offender the penalty prescribed.

Having secured the evidence they desired, the conspirators repaired to the royal presence and made accusation against Daniel. Darius at once realized the mistake he had made, and we are told he "laboured till the going down of the sun to deliver him" (v. 14). But the unhappy ruler found himself helpless in the hands of his crafty advisers. He had to own the authenticity of the decree and of his signature. He could do no other than see that it was enforced. In this we see one great point of difference between the head of gold and the silver breast. Nebuchadnezzar's word was absolute. No law held him in check: "Whom he would he slew; and whom he would he kept alive" (5:19). But it was otherwise with the Persian rulers. The law of the state had authority even over kings. And in each empire that followed we find imperial power more and more curtailed, and the voice of the people making itself heard with ever greater force and intensity until the days of the feet of the image, part of iron and part of brittle pottery—a union of social democracy and imperialism.

Darius found it impossible to evade the statute in the face of his insistent ministers, who demanded that the decree be carried out and the chief of the presidents be cast into the den of lions. The king seems to have had some sense in his soul of the power of the God of Daniel, for, after giving the command, he said to him confidently, "Thy God whom thou servest continually, he will deliver thee" (v. 16).

So Daniel was cast in, and Darius had a bad night of it, tossed between conflicting emotions of hope and fear as to his servant's fate. In the morning we see him early at the mouth of the den and in great distress calling to find out whether Daniel had been destroyed or delivered. "O Daniel, servant of the living God, is thy God, whom thou servest continually, able to deliver thee from the lions?" (v. 20)—his anxious query bespeaking both a measure of confidence in what he must have learned from Daniel himself as to the omnipotent power of his God, and yet his own lack of acquaintance with Him. But, to his joy, he found that

Daniel's God was as good as His word and had preserved the prophet unharmed in the midst of the ravenous beasts. Daniel's reply is noble in its very simplicity: "O king, live for ever," he says (v. 21). "My God hath sent his angel, and hath shut the lions' mouths, that they have not hurt me: forasmuch as before Him innocency was found in me; and also before thee, O king, have I done no hurt" (v. 22).

The misguided king is delighted to find that his own wretched blunder had wrought no real damage to his minister, and at once commands him to be taken up out of the den—the law having been complied with fully, and the prophet having suffered no hurt. Thus was Daniel delivered, "because he believed in his God" (v. 23). What a lesson to tried saints everywhere! "Who is he that will harm you, if ye be followers of that which is good?" (1 Peter 3:13). It may not always please God to deliver *from* the trial, but He will always preserve *in* it, and eventually bring His own in peace *out of* it.

The king now commands that Daniel's accusers with all their households be cast into the den. It was a heathenish way of visiting retribution upon them, inasmuch as the wives and children were not offenders, but it was quite in keeping with oriental conceptions of justice. The lions had the mastery of them, we are told, and broke all their bones in pieces the moment they came to the bottom of the den. Thus was the righteous one delivered out of trouble, while the wicked suffered in his stead.

Darius then made a new decree, which was sent to all people, nations, and languages in the Medo-Persian dominions, in which he bade men everywhere to tremble and fear before the God of Daniel: "For he is the living God, and stedfast for ever, and his kingdom that which shall not be destroyed, and his dominion shall be even unto the end. He delivereth and rescueth, and he worketh signs and wonders in heaven and in earth, who hath delivered Daniel from the power of the lions" (vv. 26–27). We may hope that Darius had thus learned the same lesson that had been taught to Nebuchadnezzar in so different a school long before. As for Daniel, the record says, he prospered in the reign of Darius and in the reign of Cyrus the Persian. How much his influence had to do with the issuing of the decree later on, permitting the Jews to return to Jerusalem, we know not, but there can be little doubt that his voice would be heard by Cyrus in the matter.

It will be necessary now to dwell somewhat particularly upon the typical character of all this. The whole scene points us on to a time when Daniel's people will once more be restored to their land, and there shall rise up among them one who will magnify himself above all that is called God and is worshiped, so that he shall sit in the temple of God showing himself that he is God. He will make a decree that prayer and worship shall be addressed to him alone and every other god ignored. All this will be considered in its place when we come to take up the latter part of chapter 11 where, from the thirty-sixth verse on, we have a vivid description of the Antichrist and his times. I do not touch here on the notion common to many Protestants that the papacy is the Antichrist because that, too, will be taken up then. What I especially wish to make clear now is that God's Word has distinctly foretold the regathering of the Jews to Palestine, though at first in unbelief, and that out of the whole company a remnant will be taken up in grace and turned to the Lord. The mass will own the claims of the willful one, who will pose as their Messiah, while the remnant will be distinguished by their unyielding opposition to his decrees and, therefore, as in the case of Daniel in this chapter, will be called upon to pass through a period of severe testing, designated in both Testaments as *the* Tribulation. But out of it all they shall eventually emerge in triumph through the power of God, and they shall see visited upon their enemies the desolation and destruction which they had thought to visit upon this faithful remnant.

And first, in order that it may be made plain that the restoration of Israel, so frequently referred to by the prophets, is yet in the future, I would direct your attention to the eleventh chapter of the prophet Isaiah. You will do well to read the entire chapter at your leisure, though I shall here quote but a few verses, beginning with the eleventh.

> And it shall come to pass in that day, that the Lord shall set his hand again the second time to recover the remnant of his people, which shall be left, from Assyria, and from Egypt, and from Pathros, and from Cush, and from Elam, and from Shinar, and from Hamath, and from the islands of the sea. And he shall set up an ensign for the natikns, and shall assemble the outcasts of Israel, and gather together the dispersed of Judah from the four corners of the earth. . . . And there shall be an highway for the remnant of his people, which shall be left, from Assyria; like as it was to Israel in the day that he came up out of the land of Egypt. (Isaiah 11:11–12, 16)

That this passage has no reference to the return from Babylon in the *past* is evident, for it distinctly tells us that the Lord shall set His hand *the second time* to recover the remnant of His people. The first time was when they came up from the dominions of Cyrus and Artaxerxes, in the days of Ezra and Nehemiah. The second recovery will be when they are brought back, not only from those lands, but from Egypt and all the islands of the sea. How they will return is set before us in the eighteenth chapter of the same prophet. There we learn that some great maritime nation will further the work of restoration by bringing them in many ships from the most distant places to their ancient patrimony. "In that time shall the present be brought unto the LORD of hosts of a people scattered and peeled, and from a people terrible from their beginning hitherto; a nation meted out and trodden under foot, whose land the rivers have spoiled, to the place of the name of the LORD of hosts, the mount Zion" (Isa. 18:7).

That this return must be carried out in order to fulfill the promises made by God to the fathers should be self-evident. In Jeremiah 30 the Lord corroborates the word in Isaiah by saying, "For, lo, the days come, saith the LORD, that I will bring again the captivity of my people Israel and Judah, saith the LORD: and I will cause them to return to the land that I gave to their fathers, and *they shall possess it"* (v. 3). And this return is still in the future, for in connection with it the pledge is given that when Jacob shall return he "shall be in rest, and be quiet, and none shall make him afraid" (Jer. 30:10). This could hardly be said of the previous return from Babylon. For at no time, until again cast out of their land after Messiah's rejection, did they dwell in rest and quietness undisturbed by their enemies and possess the land. But they are Jehovah's people, in spite of all their sins, and in His own time He will fulfill to the letter every pledge He has made. That they will have to pass through a season of severe testing before entering into the promised rest is equally clear, as the same chapter and many another portion of Scripture witnesses.

> For thus saith the LORD: We have heard a voice of trembling, of fear, and not of peace. Ask ye now, and see whether a man doth travail with child? wherefore do I see every man with his hands on his loins, as a woman in travail, and all faces are turned into paleness? Alas! for that day is great, so that none is like it: it is even the time of Jacob's trouble; but he shall be saved out of it. (Jeremiah 30:5–7)

We may turn back to Isaiah 24 for a fuller description of this time of trouble, the Great Tribulation. The first twelve verses picture the land of Palestine as it will be in those days of distress. Throughout the chapter read "land" instead of "earth." Now, notice verses 13–14: "When thus it shall be in the midst of the land among the people, there shall be as the shaking of an olive tree, and as the gleaning grapes when the vintage is done. They shall lift up their voice, they shall sing for the majesty of the LORD, they shall cry aloud from the sea." Here we have the remnant distinguished from the mass. Instead of being overwhelmed with despair because of their sorrows when cast, as it were, into this den of lions, they lift up their voices in song, like Daniel glorifying the God of heaven. To them will be fulfilled the precious promises of Isaiah 43, in the day that the Lord shall "say to the north, Give up; and to the south, Keep not back: bring my sons from far, and my daughters from the ends of the earth; even every one that is called by my name: for I have created him for my glory, I have formed him; yea, I have made him" (vv. 6–7). These shall be Jehovah's witnesses, testifying to the power and glory of the one true God when apostate Christendom shall have been given up to the strong delusion to believe the lie of the Antichrist.

The prophet Ezekiel, in chapter 36, foretells both their scattering and their regathering. Verse 24 says, "For I will take you from among the heathen, and gather you out of all countries, and will bring you into your own land." The verses that follow show us that at that time they will be cleansed from their filthiness, a new heart and a new spirit given them, the Spirit of God put within them, who will cause them to walk in His statutes and keep His judgments to do them. Now I ask any unprejudiced person, has this ever been fulfilled in the past? When the remnant of Judah returned from Babylon, did they give any evidence of having been as a company regenerated, so that they found delight in the law of the Lord? Was not the contrary the case, as evidenced by their turning away from His statutes even in the life-time of Ezra and his colaborers, and their crucifixion later of the Lord of glory?

The New Testament revelations on this subject show us plainly that their recovery awaits the close of the present dispensation. In our Lord's prophecy concerning the destruction of Jerusalem, as related Luke 21, He says, "When ye shall see Jerusalem compassed with armies, then know that the desolation thereof is nigh. . . . And they shall fall by the edge of the sword, and shall be led away captive into all the nations: and Jerusalem shall be trodden down by the Gentiles, *until* the times of the Gentiles be fulfilled" (vv. 20, 24). Jerusalem's rehabilitation awaits, then, the falling of the Stone upon the feet of the Gentile image, for, as we have already seen, that will conclude the Gentile times.

But now a connected passage in Romans 11 will show us just where and when to place the turning of the remnant to God. In verse 25 of that chapter the apostle writes, "For I would not, brethren, that ye should be ignorant of this mystery, lest ye should be wise in your own conceits; that blindness in part is happened to Israel, until the fulness of the Gentiles be come in." Now we are not to confound the fullness of the Gentiles with the *times* of the Gentiles. The latter expression takes in the entire course of Gentile domination in the Holy Land. As long as the Jew is not master in Palestine, the times of the Gentiles are running on. But the fullness of the Gentiles, as the context in this chapter makes clear, is an expression referring to spiritual blessing, not national nor temporal. This fullness will have come in when the message of the gospel has accomplished the purpose for which it was given, and God has completed His present work of taking out from among the Gentiles a people for His name. In other words, the fullness of the Gentiles and the rapture of the church are coincident.[1] Therefore, between the fullness of the Gentiles and the close of the times of the Gentiles there will be a time period in which the great bulk of prophecy will have its fulfillment. This is the period designated in Daniel "the time of the end." A reference to the chart will help to make clear its proper position. The line running across the chart beneath the parenthetic portion, which represents the present age, sets forth the fullness of the Gentiles. The line below, immediately above the inscription concerning the kingdom, represents the close of the times of the Gentiles. Between these two lines we have the time of the end. It is then that the conversion and testing of the Remnant will take place.

The later chapters of Zechariah have much to tell us of that time of trouble, and the testimony that will be maintained in it. I refer you now to but two verses:

> And it shall come to pass, that in all the land, saith the LORD, two parts therein shall be cut off and die; but the third shall be left therein. And I will bring the third part through the fire, and will refine them as silver is refined, and will try them as gold is tried: they shall call on my name, and I will hear them: I will say, It is my people: and they shall say, The LORD is my God. (Zechariah 13:8–9)

The greater part of the book of Revelation, from chapter 4 to the end of chapter 19, is concerned with the events of this time of the end. The saints seen on earth at that time are not Christians, but Jews, who will then be called upon to suffer for the sake of their once-rejected Messiah. I grant that in chapter 7, after the account of the sealed 144,000 out of all the tribes of Israel, we have pictured a great multitude whom no man can number of saved Gentiles. But they do not form part of the church nor do they appear throughout the book as in the place of testimony on earth. They come out of the Great Tribulation emerging at last to take their place in the world kingdom of our God and His Christ, but it is to the Israelite remnant alone that a place of testimony is given.[2] This remnant will then heed the Word of the Lord. They will search the Scripture and from them they will learn of their place in the course of time. They will understand that the fullness of the Gentiles has come in and that God is again taking up His earthly people. I have no doubt that this very book of Daniel that we are studying will show them where they are, and will lead them to seek the face of God and to stand for Him when all Christendom and the bulk of their own nation shall have gone into the last great apostasy. Through them a final call will go out to the heathen who have never yet heard the gospel nor rejected its precious message. The result of that ministry will be the ingathering of the great multitude shown to us in the seventh chapter of Revelation.

With this I close the present lecture and urge each one to search the Scripture for himself to see whether these things be so.

LECTURE 7

THE FOUR GREAT WORLD EMPIRES AND THE WESTERN LITTLE HORN

Daniel 7

W e now enter upon the second part of our book, and in this chapter we have a new beginning, as you will readily see by referring to the chart. Chapter 7 covers practically the same ground as chapter 2. It takes in the whole course of the times of the Gentiles, beginning with Babylon and ending in the overthrow of all derived authority and the establishment of the kingdom of the Son of Man. But the difference between the first and second divisions is this: in what we have already gone over we have been chiefly occupied with prophetic history as viewed from man's standpoint, but in the second half of the book we have the same scenes as viewed in God's unsullied light. In the second chapter, when a Gentile king had a vision of the course of world empire, he saw the image of a man—a stately and noble figure—that filled him with such admiration that he set up a similar statue to be worshiped as a god. But in this opening chapter of the second division, Daniel, the man of God, has a vision of the same empires, and he sees them as four ravenous wild beasts of so brutal a character and so monstrous withal that no actual creatures known to man could adequately set them forth.

There is something exceedingly solemn in this. If you read history as viewed simply by the natural man, you will find that a great deal of space is given to congratulating humanity upon their marvelous exploits, and one would suppose that we have now almost reached perfection, so far as human government or political economy is concerned. Civilization and the progress of the race are presumably at the zenith of their glory. But if one reads history in the light of Holy Scripture, with the Spirit of God illuminating the page, it gives one a very different impression indeed. We then begin to realize that the things that are most highly esteemed among men are abominations in the sight of God. Concerning the great ones of the earth who wield power over the nations, we are reminded of what is written in Psalm 49:12: "Man being in honour abideth not: he is like the beasts that perish."

In Daniel's visions he was given to see the course of each of the empires which these wild beasts figure. That is, each wild beast is of such a character as to picture the leading features in the entire history of the empire which it represents. For instance, the whole course of Babylon is set forth in the winged lion, which afterward had its wings plucked, a man's heart given to it, and was made to stand erect upon its feet. Then the whole course of Medo-Persia is pictured in the vision of the bear with three ribs in its mouth that lifted itself up on one side. The entire history of the Grecian Empire and its fourfold division is set forth in the four-headed and winged leopard. And the course of the Roman Empire right on down to the time of the end (a condition which has not yet been reached) is depicted in the beast, dreadful and terrible, with the great iron teeth and the ten horns. It is important to see this. Some take it for granted that, as the Roman Empire has passed off the scene, all that is connected with this Roman beast is gone, too, and so it has no further interest for us who live in the gospel dispensation. But the contrary is the truth.

But now, for a moment, look at the verse 17. There the four beasts are said to be "four kings which shall arise out of the earth." The context makes it plain, however, that the angel did not mean four individual kings, but in prophetic Scripture the term "king" is very frequently used for "kingdom." In verse 23 we read, "The fourth beast shall be the fourth *kingdom* upon the earth." Necessarily the principle applies to all. Though, on the other hand, I would have you notice that in connection with each of them, one king comes out prominently—in each case but the last, the one under whom the kingdom first attains the dignity of a great world power. Thus Nebuchadnezzar comes before us as the one who stands distinctively for Babylon, just as he was told in chapter 2, "Thou art this head of gold" (v. 38). But the winged lion represents both the glory and debasement of the Chaldean Empire. Its wings were plucked, it lost its lion heart, and was given instead the weak heart of a man. Cyrus the Great is the leading figure when we think of Medo-Persia. He it was who destroyed the chief cities of Babylon, of which the three ribs in the mouth of the bear seem to speak. The leopard clearly suggests Alexander the Great, the four wings speaking of the almost incredible swiftness of his conquests. But the four heads set forth the fourfold division of his dominions made among his leading generals after his death. But no great potentate in the past epitomizes in himself the Roman authority. We look to the future for one to arise who shall do this—even "the Beast" described in Revelation 13, who will obtain sway over Europe just prior to the establishment of the kingdom of the Son of Man, when all authority, power, and glory will be headed up in our Lord Jesus Christ.

Though these kingdoms are successive in their rising, one does not necessarily completely destroy the other; but the four great monarchies, with their characteristic features, are to run on in some form until Jesus comes. Until the dawning of that glorious morning without clouds, this world will never be free from strife and bloodshed, pestilence, misgovernment, and kindred ills. All these things, Scripture shows us, are going to continue, while evil in the professing church will increase and abound until the long-looked-for hour of the establishment of the liberty of the glory.

Sometimes people say, "I do not see how you can charitably desire the Son of God to come back the second time if it is really true that when He returns the day of grace will be over for those who have rejected His Word." But we know that the only hope of this poor world is the return of the true King. Matters will never be put right down here until they are put right by judgment. The preaching of the gospel is never going to establish the kingdom, nor did God intend that it should. After nineteen hundred years of gospel preaching, there are far more heathen in the world than there were when the Lord Jesus Christ appeared the first time. Those who are really Christians are just a little handful compared with the multitude that know not God. The gospel is not God's way of bringing in the kingdom and converting the world. This will be brought about only through judgment. While we shrink from the awful thought of what is coming upon this poor scene, yet we realize it is the only way to the blessing creation is groaning for. So we cry, "Come, Lord Jesus," for we know that He is the only hope for its deliverance. Every conflict between nations, every struggle between class interests, every cruelty that is practiced upon the weak and defenseless—all these things lead us to cry, "Come, Lord Jesus." For when He comes, He is going to put an end to it all. When He comes, He is going to dry the tears of the oppressed. When He comes, He is going to give men a righteous rule, as Daniel saw pictured in the last of these visions. First, the four world kingdoms, all of a brutish character, must run their course. Then, upon the utter breakdown of power in the hands of man, the world kingdom of the Christ of God is to be set up, when righteousness shall cover the earth as the waters cover the sea. And we may rest assured that our Lord will not come while there is one soul out of Christ who is yet anxious to be saved.

Notice that the first three beasts are passed over in the interpretation given to Daniel. It has to do almost entirely with the fourth beast, dreadful and terrible; for this beast was to be in control both at the first and second advent of our Lord.

But I now desire to notice the whole chapter a little more carefully. It was in the first year of Belshazzar, king of Babylon, that Daniel had a dream and visions of his head upon his bed. He saw the four winds of the heavens striving upon the great sea. The great sea was, of course, the Mediterranean, and it is well known that every one of the empires described in the prophecy borders upon the shores of the great sea. The kingdom of Babylon embraced the shores that stretched along the eastern and southeastern edge of the Mediterranean; Medo-Persia did the same, while Greece took in also the northeastern shores, and the Roman Empire completely surrounded it; hence its name, meaning "midst of the earth." That was the sea Daniel was looking upon in his vision, and in a very real literal sense every one of these empires seems to spring up from the great sea.

But if we turn over to Revelation 17—a book which dovetails prophetically with the book of Daniel—we get a mystic interpretation of the sea. In verse 15 we read, "He saith unto me, The waters which thou sawest, where the [harlot] sitteth, are peoples, and multitudes, and nations, and tongues." Isaiah, too, tells us that the wicked are like the troubled sea when it cannot rest, whose waters cast up mire and dirt. So we are clearly justified in interpreting the sea as a picture of the troubled nations. In other words, out of the unsettled state of the nations surrounding the Mediterranean Sea these great empires should arise.

The four winds striving upon the sea would indicate providential agencies working upon the minds of the people. You will find the figure of the winds also used in that way in the book of Revelation. Of course, though men little realize it, all the great movements of the nations are in accordance with the actings of God's providence. Thus, in a very real sense, as another has aptly said, "All history is His story." No matter what the movements going on among men, God is above them all. He may be hidden behind the scenes, but, as shown so clearly in the book of Esther, He is moving all the scenes that He is behind.

In the rise of Babylon to the dignity of the first dominion, we see the providence of God working among the nations to take away royalty from Judah because of their sins. The race lapsing into idolatry after the Flood, God committed the headship to Abraham. But when Abraham's seed violated the covenant, He took up Nebuchadnezzar and set him over all nations. But he also failed, though brought to own the power and mercy of God at last.

In his vision Daniel saw four great beasts coming up from the sea, diverse one from another. The first was like a lion and had eagles' wings—speaking of majesty, ferocity, and swiftness. It was in a marvelously short space of time that Babylon subdued all the surrounding nations and brought them beneath its sway. But as Daniel looked he saw the wings plucked, and the beast lifted up from the earth and made to stand upon the feet as a man and a man's heart given to it. Thus all progress was at an end and majesty had departed, for one can scarcely think of anything more awkward and ungainly than a lion thus erect. The heart of a man tells of weakness such as we see displayed in Belshazzar. In fact, after Nebuchadnezzar's death declension at once set in, and continued until the days when the Medes and Persians wrested the kingdom from his inglorious grandson. When this vision was given to Daniel, the last stage had almost been reached—Belshazzar was already reigning.

In the second instance Daniel saw a beast like to a bear come up from the sea, that raised itself up on one side. It had three ribs in its mouth between its teeth, and a voice said, "Arise, devour much flesh" (v. 5). It was after the decay of the Babylonian Empire that the Medo-Persian union was consummated. At first Media was the stronger, but it soon become evident that the Persians were to have the superior place. Thus the bear raised itself up on one side. The three ribs between the teeth speak of its having already destroyed its prey. It had destroyed the Babylonian lion, and the three ribs might stand for the three chief cities of the Chaldean Empire—Babylon, Ecbatana, and Borsippa, which were all taken by the united armies of Cyrus and Cyaxarea. The command to arise and devour much flesh indicates the extreme cruelties often practiced by the Persians and the wide extent of their conquests.

The third beast had the appearance of a leopard with four wings of a fowl upon its back and with four heads. It sets forth a synopsis of the history of the Grecian Empire. Something over three hundred years before Christ, Alexander the Great, as he is now known, was born as heir to Philip of Macedon. This was but one of the petty kingdoms of Greece. But after Alexander's accession to the throne, Macedon, and through it all Greece, took a place in the affairs of the world and of nations that it had never taken before. He welded together the Grecian states and Asiatic kingdoms of the West. Then he turned eastward where he met and subdued the haughty Persians completely, caused himself to be proclaimed emperor of the world, and had divine honors paid him. But his glory was short-lived, for he died as a result of licentious living and debauchery in his early thirties. His dominions were shortly afterward divided among his four leading generals. The marvelous progress of Alexander—even greater than that of Nebuchadnezzar—is indicated in the vision, for the beast that stood for Babylon had *two* wings, while the Grecian leopard had *four.*

There is an interesting story related by Josephus to the effect that when Alexander was marching through Syria, after the conquest of Tyre, with his armies headed toward Jerusalem, which he intended to destroy, the high priest and his companions robed themselves in their priestly garments and marched in solemn procession out of the city to meet the conqueror. Alexander is said to have recognized the high priest as one whom he had seen in a vision. From his hand he received a copy of this book of Daniel, in which the prophecies concerning himself were pointed out. Because of what was there written, he accepted the submission of the Jews, granted them religious toleration, and left their city unharmed. While we have no means now of deciding as to the truth or falsity of this story, we can readily see that it is not at all unlikely.

The fourth beast is described in verses 7–8:

> After this I saw in the night visions, and behold a fourth beast, dreadful and terrible, and strong exceedingly; and it had great iron teeth: it devoured and brake in pieces, and stamped the residue with the feet of it: and it was diverse from all the beasts that were before it; and it had ten horns. I considered the horns, and, behold, there came up among them another little horn, before whom there were three of the first horns plucked up by the roots: and, behold, in this horn were eyes like the eyes of a man, and a mouth speaking great things.

In its turn, the Grecian Empire was overthrown, and, about half a century before Christ, Rome became the mistress of the world. The very birth of the Lord Jesus in Bethlehem was brought about, humanly speaking, by a decree going forth from Caesar Augustus that all the world should be taxed (registered for a census). This brought Mary and her husband Joseph to the city of David, foretold by Micah as the birthplace of Him "whose goings forth have been from of old, from everlasting" (5:2). Upon the chart, I have represented this beast as of a composite character, for I take it that it answers to the beast described in Revelation 13 as having the head of a lion, the body of a leopard, and the feet of a bear, thus including in itself the chief features of all the kingdoms pictured by the other beasts. It was the boast of the Romans that they never destroyed a civilization when they conquered the people, but they took from it everything of merit and, combining all into one, produced the greatest civilization the world had ever known. The course of this last beast has not yet been fully run. In the book of Revelation, it is described as having seven heads, one of which was wounded to death and afterward healed. The seven heads are said to be seven kings or forms of government. In John's day, five had already passed away; the sixth or imperial form, was then in existence. The other had not yet come, nor has it appeared up to the present time. It will have its fulfillment in the union of imperialism and democracy, which we have already seen is to take place in the time of the end. But as the interpretation of this vision is given farther on in the chapter, we will not go into it now.

Daniel next saw thrones set up. You will notice that the Authorized Version says, "The thrones were *cast down*" (v. 9). This literally renders the Chaldean expression here used which implies the casting down of rugs and cushions to be used as an oriental divan throne. But the English translation would seem to imply the *destruction* of thrones, so it is better rendered "set up." He continues, "And the Ancient of days did sit, whose garment was white as snow, and the hair of his head like the pure wool: his throne was like the fiery flame, and his wheels as burning fire. A fiery stream issued and came forth from before him: thousand thousands ministered unto him, and ten thousand times ten thousand stood before him: the judgment was set, and the books were opened" (vv. 9–10). Daniel then saw that because of the blasphemous words of the little horn, the last beast was slain and his body destroyed and given to the burning flame. The other beasts had not been dealt with so summarily. They had their dominion taken away, but a prolonging in life was given them, as the margin puts it, thus agreeing with what we know as to their history.

The Son of Man is then seen coming with the clouds of heaven unto the Ancient of Days, who gives him "dominion, and glory, and a kingdom, that all people, nations, and languages, should serve him: his dominion is an everlasting dominion, which shall not pass away, and His kingdom that which shall not be destroyed" (v. 14). This completes the vision. The interpretation follows.

Daniel was deeply exercised in spirit over all that he had seen, but an angel seems to have been standing by and to him he applied for light as to "the truth of all this" (v. 16). He tells him that the four beasts represent four kings or kingdoms, as we have already seen, "but the saints of the most High [places] shall take the kingdom, and possess the kingdom for ever, even for ever and ever" (v. 18). But Daniel desires fuller information as to the meaning of the fourth beast, and especially of the little "horn that had eyes, and a mouth that spake very great things, whose look was more stout than his fellows" (v. 20), who rooted up three of the ten horns and "made war with the saints, and prevailed against them; until the Ancient of days came, and judgment was given to the saints of the most High [places]; and the time came that the saints possessed the kingdom" (vv. 21–22).

The angel explains that out of the fourth kingdom shall arise ten kings—clearly at one time. From among these another shall arise after them who shall be diverse from the first and shall subdue three of them. He will be characterized by blaspheming the name of the Most High. He can be none other than the Beast of Revelation 13 and 17. He will persecute the saints of the most high places—the Remnant-saints, of whom, as we have already noticed, Scripture has much to say in connection with the last days. He it is of whom we read in the ninth chapter who shall confirm a covenant with the Jews for seven years. But it is he who shall violate his covenant in the midst of the specified period as here stated, "Shall . . . think to change times and laws: and they shall be given into his hand until a time and times and the dividing of time" (v. 25), that is, he will be the persecutor of the Jewish remnant for the last three-and-a-half years of the time of the end. But at the expiration of that time, the judgment shall sit, the Lord Himself shall return from heaven, and his dominion shall be taken away, and he himself, as we learn in Revelation 19, will be cast alive into the lake of fire.

Then "the kingdom and dominion, and the greatness of the kingdom under the whole heaven, shall be given to the people of the saints of the most High, whose kingdom is an everlasting kingdom, and all dominions shall serve and obey him" (v. 27). Thus will be brought in that everlasting kingdom for which the groaning earth has been waiting so long.

I am quite aware that there are many interpreters who think they see in the little horn, as in the king of 11:36, the papacy, which pretended to universal dominion after the downfall of the Roman Empire. But the little horn is not to rise up until after that empire has reached its ten-kingdom condition, and this we have already observed has never been the case in the past. At no time after the dismemberment of the empire did ten kingdoms formed from its fragments unite in one. And then it is also important to remember that the papacy existed before the breakup of the empire; so that the pope, instead of rising up upon the head of the beast after all the other horns had obtained their strength, came up before the ten horns existed at all, which is clearly contrary to what is here stated as to the blaspheming little horn. And it is further to be observed that the little horn is wielding supreme power on earth at the coming of the Son of Man to set up His kingdom, whereas it is evident that the papacy has not been supreme, nor indeed recognized, as a world power for many years.

In the Revelation, the papal church is represented by the scarlet woman riding the beast, but, in the time of the end, the ten horns are to unite in seeking and carrying out her destruction. Notice carefully that in Revelation 17:12–13 it is written, "And the ten horns which thou sawest are ten kings, which have received no kingdom as yet; but receive power as kings *one hour with the beast.* These have one mind and shall give their power and strength unto the beast." Whereas in verse 16 we learn that their power shall be used for the destruction of Babylon the Great: "And the ten horns which thou sawest *and* [not upon] the beast, these shall hate the [harlot], and shall make her desolate and naked, and shall eat her flesh, and burn her with fire." Thus it should be plain to any careful reader that the little horn of Daniel is the Roman beast of Revelation, and that he will be acknowledged as supreme arbiter of Europe in the coming day of tribulation by the ten kingdoms. He will be permitted to prosper and to persecute the faithful remnant of Israel after the church has been translated to heaven until the appearing of the Lord Jesus Christ with all His saints for the destruction of those who have refused His Word.

It is with the events of this brief season, called "the time of the end," that the great bulk of prophecy has to do. The present age is one never referred to in the Old Testament, save in the most general way. For the calling out of the church was a mystery hidden in God throughout all past ages and only revealed in this dispensation for the obedience of faith. The church may now be completed at any moment, and then the next great event will be the descent of the Lord in the air and the translation of His bride, thus preparing the way for the things that are coming upon the earth.

In the last verse of our chapter, Daniel tells us that he kept these things in his heart. May we do the same. Surely, as Christians, nothing will give us to understand our own present place and portion so well as to have a clear apprehension of the place that Israel and the nations have in the mind of God, as revealed in His Word. In the present age it should be accounted a happy privilege to pass through this scene as strangers and pilgrims, sharing with Christ in His rejection. For us, this is the time to suffer for righteousness' sake—the time to rejoice if accounted worthy to endure shame for His name's sake. The glory is coming when He returns to take His great power and reign. Until then, be it ours to "go forth . . . unto him without the camp, bearing his reproach" (Heb. 13:13).

O unsaved one, it is well that you too ponder these things in your heart, that you be not blinded by the false and deceitful glare of the tinseled glory of this world. It is all doomed to pass away, and unhappy will be your lot if you, in that day, have no interests in a more stable scene. "The things which are seen are temporal; but the things which are [unseen] are eternal" (2 Cor. 4:18). See to it, I plead with you, that you are numbered among those who have part in the everlasting kingdom so soon to succeed all the passing dominions of this world. God has, in grace, given His Son to die for your salvation. But remember that it is written, "As it is appointed unto men once to die, but after this the judgment: so Christ was once offered to bear the sins of many; and unto them that look for him shall he appear the second time without sin unto salvation" (Heb. 9:27–28). If you would hail His promised advent with joy, you must know Him now as Savior. Otherwise His return to this earth to reign would find you numbered among His enemies to be destroyed from before His face.

LECTURE 8

THE GRECIAN LITTLE HORN

Daniel 8

In beginning this address, I would call your attention to a most interesting fact in regard to the structure of the book we are considering. It was originally written in two languages. The first chapter and verses 1–3 of chapter 2 are in Hebrew. But from verse 4 of the second chapter to the end of chapter 7, the language employed is Chaldean, or Aramaic. The balance of the book is in Hebrew. There seems to be a very simple and yet significant reason for this. The first section was for the special help and encouragement of the faithful among the scattered Jews, so it was written in their own language. But in the second section, God is tracing out the course of the times of the Gentiles, and He led Daniel to write the record of it in the popular language of the day that the Chaldeans might read it understandingly and profit thereby.

The portion to which we now turn, beginning with this eighth chapter and going on to the end of the book, concerns the Jews in a very special way, so it was written in Hebrew, as was the first part. It is of importance to see the different applications of each of these sections. God has nothing to say about the course of Christendom or the church of this dispensation either here or elsewhere in the Prophets. He is giving us the truth both in regard to Judah and Israel and to the Gentiles as such. If we fail to observe this, Scripture will be all in confusion;

76

that is, *our apprehension* of it. The principle is a simple one but, if kept in mind, will aid greatly to a proper understanding of the Word of God.

When in the Prophets we read of Judah, we are not to suppose the church is meant, nor yet when we read of Zion or of Jerusalem. Judah means Judah, Zion means Zion, Jerusalem means Jerusalem, Israel means Israel, and the Gentiles have neither part nor lot in what is written concerning these. The church, which is the body of Christ, is something very different. There are three, not merely two, classes of people in the world today—all contemplated in Scripture. "Give none offence," says the apostle Paul, in writing to the Corinthians, "neither to the Jews, nor to the Gentiles, nor to the church of God" (1 Cor. 10:32). These are the three classes. If the various passages of Scripture referring to each are rightly divided and not all mixed up together in the mind of the reader, he is in a fair way to get a proper understanding of what is commonly called dispensational truth, which is nothing more nor less than giving to each dispensation or period of God's special dealings with men the portions that apply particularly to each.

In studying the Chaldean part of this book we have noticed how the omniscient God has traced for us the course of the great empires of this world. We have had outlined for our learning their rise, progress, decline, and fall, emphasizing the truth that "righteousness exalteth a nation: but sin is a reproach to any people" (Prov. 14:34). Now all this was written in the language spoken by the Gentiles at that time. But we are now to be largely occupied with that race long-despised and hated but ever watched over by Jehovah—His covenant people of old, beloved for the fathers' sakes, no matter how great their failure and sin. That is why the last part of the book is written in Hebrew. It is true that we shall still read of some of these world powers (we are largely occupied with two of them in this chapter), but it is only as clearing the ground for light in regard to the future of the Jewish nation.

A careful study of the book of Revelation will show you that it is very similar in structure to the book of Daniel. After the first part (Rev. 1–3), which is devoted to the prophetic history of the church, we have from chapter 4 through 11:18 the judgments that are to fall upon apostate Christendom and the powers connected with it. Their history is traced right on down to the end, closing with "the time of the dead, that they should be judged" (Rev. 11:18). But the Lord had said to John: "Thou must prophesy again" (Rev. 10:11). So he begins to take things up once more from chapter 12 on, but it is all connected with God's earthly people, the nation of Israel.[1] Thus the first part has chiefly to do with the course of the world as such, and it turns the divine searchlight upon the great movements among the nations. But the second half has to do with the same people that we have before us in the last part of Daniel. As remarked in the previous address, the one book dovetails into the other. Daniel cannot be understood apart from the book of the Revelation, and Revelation itself is in many places only intelligible because of what had previously been made known to the prophet in Babylon. Let us remember then that our present chapter is the first of the Hebrew section, while the chapters we have lately been reading were in Aramaic, and especially concerned the Gentiles.

The first verse shows us that two years elapsed between the visions of chapter 7 and what we have here, for it was in the third year of the reign of king Belshazzar that Daniel was given the vision of the ram and the he-goat. Either actually or in spirit, he was in the palace, in the province of Elam by the river Ulai. Elam was the ancient name of the highlands east of Babylon, stretching from India to the Persian Gulf. It was in this very region that Cyrus was to obtain his first great victories. So it was fitting that in his vision Daniel should be in the land soon to be completely dominated by the Persians, because that which he saw had largely to do with Persia in her early triumphs and subsequent defeat.

He tells us that he lifted up his eyes, "and saw, and, behold, there stood before the river a ram which had two horns: and the two horns were high; but one was higher than the other, and the higher came up last. I saw the ram pushing westward, and northward, and southward; so that no beasts might stand before him, neither was there any that could deliver out of his hand; but he did according to his will, and became great" (vv. 3–4). In verse 15 we have drawing near the interpreting angel whose mission it was to explain the meaning of the vision. We shall notice each part separately, connecting with it the interpretation given. In verses 19–20, the angel says, "Behold, I will make thee know what shall be in the last end of the indignation: for at the time appointed the end shall be. The ram which thou sawest having two horns are the kings of Media and Persia." Thus we are not left to form our own judgment as to what the ram might represent, but we are distinctly told by the angel that it stands for the same dominion as the breast and arms of silver in Nebuchadnezzar's great image, and the bear that was lifted up on one side in the previous vision. It is as though God would give us symbol after symbol to impress upon our minds the events to follow one another upon the earth prior to the establishment of the kingdom of His Son. "A threefold cord," we are told elsewhere, "is not quickly broken" (Eccl. 4:12).

Remember that when Daniel had the vision, Babylon was still the supreme power, though already in its decline. But Daniel was given this revelation as to the ram of Persia, when no human mind could possibly have predicted the place it was to take in the affairs of men. It is rather interesting to know that, according to standard authorities, the ram was the symbol of Persia, and a picture of one was borne on her banners before her armies. The two horns, the higher of which came up last, clearly connect with the bear lifting itself up on one side. That is, they act forth the fact that the Medo-Persian Empire was composed of two nations—the ancient and venerable kingdom of Media and the then-modern kingdom of Persia, the latter of which, after the confederation, became by far the more powerful of the two. Thus the horn that came up last was the higher. Daniel saw this ram pushing westward, northward, and southward, thereby indicating exactly the course of Persian conquest. The armies of Cyrus did not turn eastward to conquer the barbarous tribes toward the sun-rising, but they pressed toward the Mediterranean and Black Seas and the Persian Gulf and continued their conquests until all western Asia and Egypt were subject to them.

While Daniel was considering what the ram could mean, he saw a he-goat come from the west on the face of the whole earth, which touched not the ground—it ran so swiftly. This goat had a notable horn between his eyes, and he came to the ram that had the two horns and ran upon him in the fury of his power. Daniel vividly describes the terrific onslaught: "And I saw him come close unto the ram, and he was moved with choler against him, and smote the ram, and brake his two horns: and there was no power in the ram to stand before him; but he cast him down to the ground, and stamped upon him: and there was none that could deliver the ram out of his hand" (v. 7).

The interpretation is given in verse 21: "The rough goat is the king of Grecia: and the great horn that is between his eyes is the first king." Thus we are again freed from all necessity of exercising any ingenuity in order to find out the meaning of the vision; for God has Himself revealed it through His angel.

Greece, at the time that Daniel prophesied, consisted of a number of independent and often warring states, bound together nevertheless by ties of consanguinity. It remained for Alexander the Third, commonly called the Great, the remarkably gifted son of Philip of Macedon, to consolidate these separate kingdoms into one loyal, united power, which was destined for a season to rule the world. Here, as everywhere in the book, the vision exactly answers to the after-history. I do not want to occupy you too much with history, for a knowledge of human records is certainly not necessary to enable one to understand the Word of God. But on the other hand nothing is gained by ignorance, and faith is but confirmed, and God glorified, when we see how the wonderful exactness of His holy Word is witnessed to by the annals of uninspired men.

The first thing of note I would have you observe is this: the he-goat came from the west. Now, according to history, we know that an altogether new thing appeared in the rise and progress of Alexander the Great. Previous to that time, power had always risen up in the east and reached out toward the west. The East was the cradle of the human race, and there the most ancient civilizations existed. The nations of the Orient thought of all the rest of the world, especially the distant lands of the west, as "barbarians," for whom they entertained a haughty contempt. But from the despised West came the he-goat with great choler. In great passion, he touched not the ground in the swiftness and the fury of his onslaught. In this it is easy to see a fitting symbol of the whirlwind campaign of the army of the west headed by its intrepid commander.

The overrunning of Asia by Alexander was not merely to gratify his ambition for world empire, but it was a paying off of old scores. The Greeks had never forgotten the disgrace and shame of earlier Persian conquests. Nor could they forgive the Persians for their unsuccessful descent, under Xerxes, upon the Hellenic States. For years they had brooded over these things and had nursed the desire for a bloody and triumphant revenge. At last they realized that the time had come to gratify their passion. Hence, it was with more than usual alacrity that they sprang to arms, and at Alexander's beck and call, rushed upon the Persian hosts in angry mood, eager to settle up these old scores and execute vengeance upon their ancient enemies. So Daniel sees the he-goat moved with power. By this terrific attack, the ram was cast to the ground and his two horns broken. All this was fulfilled when Alexander met the hosts of the last Darius and completely defeated them. By this he became ruler of the world.

But Daniel goes on to say, "The he goat waxed very great: and when he was strong, the great horn was broken; and for it came up four notable ones toward the four winds of heaven" (v. 8). In the interpretation, after explaining that the great horn was the first king of Grecia, the angel says, "Now that being broken, whereas four stood up for it, four kingdoms shall stand up out of the nation, but not in his power" (v. 22). Alexander's day of power was a very brief one, his early death testifying to his inability to hold in check his appetites and passions, and thus the great horn was broken.

None of his own house succeeded Alexander. But, upon his untimely decease, his dominions were divided among his four leading generals, namely, Ptolemy, who was acknowledged as king of Egypt and the adjacent countries; Seleucas, who took Syria and Asia Minor; Lysimachus, who had the sovereignty of Thrace and the contiguous territory; and Cassander, to whom fell Macedonia and all Greece. Thus was the empire divided, and there was never again a master hand commanding until the Roman conquest in the last century before Christ. Two of these divisions occupy a large place in prophecy.

But Scripture never again occupies us with Thrace, and only once directly with Greece, and that in Zechariah 9:13. But Syria and Egypt are the powers known in this book as the "King of the North" and the "King of the South." Directions in Scripture are always, unless otherwise specified, to be understood as having reference to Jerusalem as a center, and so, when the Bible speaks of the north and the south, it is north or south of Jerusalem. Unless this is kept in mind, one may easily become confused. Up to a little more than fifty years before the coming of the Lord Jesus, these two kingdoms existed as independent powers with the land of Palestine between them. The Holy Land thus became a veritable battleground for their opposing armies torn by dissensions for over two hundred years. The wretched history of those two centuries of horror is given us prophetically in chapter 11, and we shall take them up in detail when we come to consider that portion of the book.

The chief reason for introducing all this was that we might be enlightened in regard to one who is to play a very important part in the time of the end, and who is destined to arise out of the Syrian division of Alexander's empire. For the present, and ever since the Roman conquest, the goat with the four horns has been apparently destroyed. But just as the Roman Empire is to be revived in the last days, so we learn that two out of the four horns of the divided Grecian dominion will reappear upon the prophetic map in that time of trial, and out of one of them shall that Little Horn arise who will be the bitter enemy of the returned Jews in that day. In verses 9–12 we read:

> And out of one of them came forth a little horn, which waxed exceeding great, toward the south, and toward the east, and toward the pleasant land. And it waxed great, even to the host of heaven; and it cast down some of the host and of the stars to the ground, and stamped upon them. Yea, he magnified himself even to the prince of the host, and by him the daily sacrifice was taken away, and the place of his sanctuary was cast down. And a host was given him against the daily sacrifice by reason of transgression, and it cast down the truth to the ground; and it practised and prospered.

I do not question for a moment that all this has had a fulfillment in the enormities of that monster of wickedness, Antiochus Epiphanes, whose persecutions of the Jews and desecration of the temple are here described. But a comparison with the interpretation of the vision makes it equally clear, to my mind, that there remains another and more complete fulfillment yet to take place.

Many confound the Little Horn here spoken of with the Little Horn of chapter 7. But we have already noticed that he who rises up in the western ten-horned kingdom is the same as the Beast of Revelation 13–17. He is a Roman, not a Grecian offshoot. Here, we see one arising out of the old kingdom of Seleucas—a king of the north, not of the west. Antiochus in his bloodthirsty career was the type of one who will be Jerusalem's bitter enemy in the time of the Lord's indignation. Now the Turks have for centuries been in possession of the lands once dominated by Seleucas. The future King of the North, therefore, will in all likelihood be the last sultan of the Ottoman Empire, or the fierce leader of whatever power controls Turkey in Asia at that time.

The Roman Little Horn will be an apostate Christian in league with the personal Antichrist, who will take unbelieving Israel under his wing so long as it suits his purposes. The Grecian Little Horn is likely an utter infidel, the successor to Muhammad, actuated by inveterate hatred to the Jews, and probably the bitter foe of the future emperor of the west. The angel tells Daniel in verses 23–25,

> In the latter time of their kingdom, when the transgressors are come to the full, a king of fierce countenance, and understanding dark sentences, shall stand up. And his power shall be mighty, but not by his own power: and he shall destroy wonderfully, and shall prosper, and practice, and shall destroy the mighty and the holy people. And through his policy also he shall cause craft to prosper in his hand; and he shall magnify himself in his heart, and by peace shall destroy many: he shall also stand up against the Prince of princes; but he shall be broken without hand.

Now it is evident that much that is here written cannot possibly apply to Antiochus. He answers quite fully to the *vision,* but he does not meet the requirements of the *interpretation.* In the first place, the prophecy is to have its complete accomplishment "when the transgressors are come to the full," an expression which might refer to the ripening of iniquity in Syria of old were it not that the kingdom was not destroyed upon the death of Epiphanes, as it would have been if its sins had reached the limit set by the Moral Governor of the universe. It seems far more likely that the expression refers to the time of the end, when the whole world will be ripe for the judgment of God.

This agrees with the angel's words, "I will make thee know what shall be in the last end of the indignation" (v. 19), which is undoubtedly the end of the times of the Gentiles. In that time, then, this predicted Little Horn shall stand up, a man of great intelligence and diplomacy but of whom we read that "his power shall be mighty, but not by his own power." Now these words could hardly be applied to the "little horn" of the past, for he reigned as an independent monarch, prosecuting his purposes as his own will dictated until in measure thwarted by the interference of Rome. But there is a leader who occupies a large place in prophecy, denominated by Isaiah "the Assyrian," who will be Israel's enemy in the last days, and who is to be destroyed by the personal appearance of the Lord Jesus Christ. Israel's blessing and restoration are connected by Isaiah with his downfall. He seems clearly to be the same as the Little Horn here depicted, for he too relies, apparently, upon some other ally. The power that will back him is prophesied of in Ezekiel 38 and is evidently Russia, the great dominion of the north. Then, again, the Little Horn is to stand up against the Prince of princes and be broken without hands. The Prince of princes can be none other than the Messiah. Consequently, these words were not fulfilled in the life and death of Antiochus. But they point us on to the time of the end, when Messiah Himself shall appear in person on behalf of oppressed Israel and shall overthrow the Assyrian.

What is said of the Little Horn as an individual is largely applicable to the Ottoman Empire as a whole. Fierce and relentless, it has ever been the enemy of the people of God. It has existed for centuries, not because of any inherent power of its own, but because of the jealousies of the nations of Europe. Were the Turk driven out of Constantinople, all Europe would be thrown into war, each great power anxious to possess the dominions over which the Crescent now floats. Hence the abominable horrors of Armenian and Jewish massacres are permitted by civilized and so-called Christian nations because they do not dare to interfere, lest by so doing they jeopardize the peace of the world.[2] It is said of the Little Horn that he shall cause craft to prosper and by peace shall destroy many. This, too, has been characteristic of the "unspeakable Turk," especially in his dealings with the Jews. The monotheism of Mohammedanism naturally appeals to the Jew, and the false prophet himself made marked advances to the seed of Israel, hoping thereby to win them over to Islam. But behind all the fair words and goodly promises of the sultans, the poison and the sword have ever lurked. The Little Horn of the latter times will embody in himself the spirit of the Ottoman Empire.

But we have not yet finished with the vision. In verses 13–14, Daniel says, "Then I heard one saint speaking, and another saint said unto that certain saint which spake. How long shall be the vision concerning the daily sacrifice, and the transgression of desolation, to give both the sanctuary and the host to be trodden under foot? And he said unto me, Unto two thousand and three hundred days; then shall the sanctuary be cleansed." The word for days is really "evening-mornings," and refers, not to lengthened periods, but clearly and distinctly to twenty-four-hour days. It is a time-prophecy that has to do with the defilement of the temple by Antiochus. From the time that he polluted the sanctuary by sacrificing a sow upon the altar and setting up a statue of Jupiter in the holiest of all, twenty-three hundred literal days elapsed until it was again purified and dedicated to the service of Jehovah. As if to warn us of the danger of allegorizing this period, the angel says to Daniel in verse 26, "The vision of the evening and the morning which was told is true: wherefore shut thou up the vision; for it shall be for many days."

It was the failure to apprehend this that led the Millerites into their great blunder in the early part of the last century, and the same crude error has blinded their successors, the Seventh-Day Adventists, and resulted in the blasphemous sanctuary theory which they hold. According to them, the Lord Jesus never entered the holiest until A.D. 1844, being twenty-three hundred year-days from the time when Cyrus issued the decree to build the temple. But it is all an unhallowed nightmare, utterly unsupported by Scripture. The twenty-three hundred days have long since been fulfilled in the history of Daniel's people, the Jews, and that literally, after the desecration of the holy places by the Syrian tyrant. There is no hint that there remains another twenty-three hundred days to be fulfilled in the future, though the characters of the Little Horn of the vision and the last great Assyrian of Isaiah 14:24–27 are so very much alike. This latter will undoubtedly be a man of great ability but cunning, crafty, and deceitful—a worthy successor to the Ottoman rulers of the past. But he is to be broken in Immanuel's land, and all his army shall be destroyed upon the mountains of Israel, when he dares to stand up against the Prince of princes, who shall come forth in glorious majesty for the deliverance of the faithful remnant whose hearts will cleave to Jehovah in that dreadful Time of Jacob's Trouble. Already we can see events shaping themselves for the fulfillment of these things. The end cannot be far off. "Blessed is he that watcheth, and keepeth his garments, lest he walk naked, and they see his shame" (Rev. 16:15).

The effect of the vision on Daniel was that he fainted and was sick certain days. "Afterward," he says, "I rose up, and did the king's business; and I was astonished at the vision, but none understood it" (v. 27). The centuries since have borne witness to the truth of much of it; the days to come will manifest the balance. May our hearts be so impressed by these things that we too shall be deeply exercised before God about them, and that we may be found in a very real sense doing the King's business while we wait for His personal return from heaven!

Nor would I close without once more warning the Christless to flee from the wrath to come. The clouds of doom are gathering, black and ominous, over this poor world. Soon the lightnings of wrath, the thunders of judgment, and the storm of vengeance will break forth. How unspeakably sad will be your condition if exposed to the full fury of the tempest of the divine indignation, with no Christ, no refuge nigh! Trust Him now while grace is offered to each sinful soul; else "What wilt thou say when He shall punish thee? "

LECTURE 9

THE SEVENTY WEEKS

Daniel 9

The main feature of the chapter that is now to occupy our attention is the great prophecy of the seventy weeks. Sir Edward Denny, a noted prophetic student of the last century, used commonly to call this "the backbone of prophecy." This title seems well given, for if the seventy weeks be misunderstood, then an effort will necessarily be made to bend all the other prophetic Scripture passages into accord with that misinterpretation. But if we have a correct understanding of the teaching of this chapter, we can then see readily how all prophecy, without any forcing, falls right into place and is intimately linked up with this the greatest of all-time prophecies.

We will spend a little while first in noting what led up to the giving of this special revelation. Daniel was himself a prophetic student. He was one who realized deeply in his own soul, though the words had not yet been written, that "All Scripture is given by inspiration of God, and is profitable for doctrine, for reproof, for correction, for instruction in righteousness, that the man of God may be perfect, thoroughly furnished unto all good works" (2 Tim. 3:16–17). And so we see, in the opening verses, this devoted man in the first year of the reign of Darius bending over the prophetic word in the Holy Scripture. He did not have anything like as complete a Bible as we have, but he valued what he had

86

and searched diligently. In fact, the last book that had been added to the Bible was that of Ezekiel. We do not know for certain that this ever came into his hands, but we do know from this passage that he had, at any rate, the book of Jeremiah. As he studied it carefully, he noticed that twice in that book it was written that God would accomplish seventy years in the desolations of Jerusalem.

Now as Daniel looked back and reckoned the years he had spent in the court of Nebuchadnezzar, then the days that had followed during the period of Babylon's difficulties, succeeded by the triumph of the Medes and Persians, and counted it all up, he evidently realized that the seventy years must have very nearly run out. Therefore, the day of the deliverance of the Jews must have drawn very near. He could probably look back over almost seven decades himself, for he had been carried away as a captive in the reign of Jehoiakim when he was but a lad, and he had become an old man.

We find that the study of prophecy exercised the heart and the conscience of Daniel. He was not merely interested in it from an intellectual standpoint. The mere computing of times and seasons could not satisfy this devout man of God; but when he learned from his Bible that the time had almost drawn near for the people of Judah to be restored to their land, it stirred him to the very depths of his soul and brought him down to his knees. He might have said, "If it is God's purpose to restore His people, He will carry that purpose out, whatever their condition, and I need not concern myself about this matter." But no, Daniel realized that when God is about to work, He begins by exercising His people that they may be restored in soul if they have wandered from Him, and thus blessing would result upon their being brought into the place of self-judgment and humiliation before Him.

Happy will it be for us if the study of his book has the same effect upon us that the study of the book of Jeremiah had upon Daniel. If not, I fear it will have a hardening effect and will leave us in a worse condition than when we began. But if these things we have been going over, all that God has been bringing before us, shall result in casting us down in lowliness before Him and causing us to cry, "O Lord God, we have sinned, we have much reason to be before Thee in confession and brokenness, because of the failure of Thy people, the church of which we form a part," I say if it has this effect upon us, yea in us, it will be indeed for God's glory and our blessing.

And, surely, we have serious cause to be on our knees before God when we think of all the failure and the sin that has come in to mar our testimony. We will not feel much like finding fault with others if really before God as to our own shame in all this. Sometimes when I hear people railing against this denomination and that company of Christians, while glorying in their own position and utterly ignoring their true state, I think how little such persons enter into the thoughts and feelings that filled the heart and wrung confession from the lips of this man Daniel.

Notice that he does not begin by accusing the Jews who had acted so badly in the days gone by, nor his contemporaries at that solemn moment in Israel's history. But he sets his face unto Jehovah, to seek Him in prayer and supplication with fasting and sackcloth and ashes—the outward expression of deep and heartfelt repentance. We are told that he prayed unto the Lord his God and made his confession. He says, "We have sinned, and have committed iniquity, and have done wickedly, and have rebelled, even by departing from thy precepts and from thy judgments: neither have we harkened unto thy servants the prophets, which spake in thy name" (vv. 5–6). He owns the righteousness of God in the judgment that had come upon them. Yet he dares to plead that to the Lord his God belong mercies and forgiveness, though they had so grievously rebelled against Him. In all His dealings with them, God had but confirmed His own words and made manifest the faithfulness of His testimony through Moses His servant.

How much we may learn from all this! When we look around and see the failure in the church, the fleshliness and the worldliness that prevail on every hand, let us not be content to pass our judgment upon them, and lift up our hearts in spiritual pride and say, "Thank God, we are not as others," but oh, let us remember that we too are part of that church which has failed. We cannot dissociate ourselves from other Christians. We have to take our place with them, bow our heads in the presence of God, and own that we have sinned. If we could but remember this always, it would cure us of railing against the people of God who have less light than we have, or than we fancy that we have.

I remember a dear servant of God writing to me a number of years ago from a place where he was laboring in the gospel: "Prejudice is very strong here, and I regret to have to feel that in large measure our own dear brethren are to blame for much of it. In times past they have spent so much time stoning what, no doubt, very much deserved to be stoned, but which we have no authority to stone."[1] God has not raised us up to go around stoning His people. We have not been appointed to be the censors of Christendom. He has said, "Who art thou that judgest another man's servant? to his own master he standeth or falleth" (Rom. 14:4).

And so, as we pass on our way, let us be exercised about individual holiness and faithfulness to God, concerned too, about corporate righteousness and freedom from unholy associations. But do not let us seek to sit in judgment upon our fellow Christians who may not happen to see eye to eye with us, but whose love for the Lord Jesus and faithfulness to what they do see might be an example well worthy of our imitation. No, let us rather take Daniel's place of self-abasement and repentance in the presence of God, and throw our arms of love and faith about all His dear people and say, "O God, *we*,"—not *they*—"we have sinned and done this evil in thy sight." And when we get into that state, then we can count upon His blessing and can look to Him expectantly for a measure of recovery. It is this that shines out so beautifully in our prophet. He identifies himself, though a man of unusual faithfulness (perhaps in fact, the most devoted man of his generation), with his failed and failing nation.

In simplicity and faith he then looks up to God, beseeching Him to let His anger and His fury be turned away from Jerusalem and to cause His face to shine upon the sanctuary that was desolate. Note the earnestness and pathos of verses 18–19 with which he concludes his touching petition: "O my God, incline thine ear, and hear; open thine eyes, and behold our desolations, and the city which is called by thy name: for we do not present our supplications before thee for our righteousnesses, but for thy great mercies. O Lord, hear; O Lord, forgive; O Lord, hearken and do; defer not, for thine own sake, O my God; for thy city and thy people are called by thy name."

Prayer of such a character could not fail of an answer. While he was speaking and making his confession, the angel Gabriel, "being caused to fly swiftly, touched him about the time of the evening oblation" (v. 21)—that is, at the time when the smoking sacrifice, pointing on to the offering of our Lord Jesus Christ, would have been ascending to God had Jerusalem not been in ruins. Gabriel declares that he has been sent to give Daniel skill and understanding in regard to the times, foreknown of God, of Israel's blessing. I quote his message in full and ask you to note carefully every word.

> Seventy weeks are determined [or, cut off] upon thy people and upon thy holy city, to finish the transgression, and to make an end of sins, and to make reconciliation for iniquity, and to bring in everlasting righteousness, and to seal up the vision and prophecy, and to anoint the most Holy [or, the Holy of Holies]. Know therefore and understand, that from the going forth of the commandment to restore and to build Jerusalem unto the Messiah the Prince, shall be seven weeks, and threescore and two weeks: the street shall be built again, and the wall, even in troublous times [or, the strait, or narrow times]. And after threescore and two weeks shall Messiah be cut off, but not for himself [or, and

shall have nothing]: and the people of the prince that shall come shall destroy the city and the sanctuary; and the end thereof shall be with a flood, and unto the end of the war desolations are determined [or, until the end shall be war and desolations as determined]. And he shall confirm the covenant with many for one week: and in the midst of the week he shall cause the sacrifice and the oblation to cease, and for the overspreading of abominations he shall make it desolate [or, upon the wing of abominations shall come one who maketh desolate], even until the consummation, and that determined shall be poured upon the desolate [or, desolator]. (vv. 24–27)

Now in considering this prophecy in detail, it is important, first of all, to notice that the time period of seventy weeks clearly refers to years. Daniel had been learning from the Scriptures that the Lord would accomplish seventy years in the desolations of Jerusalem. But in answer to his prayer God makes known to him that in seventy weeks, or sevens of years, all prophecy in connection with His people Israel will be fulfilled. The word here rendered "weeks" does not necessarily mean weeks of days, but it is a generic term (like our word *dozen*) a *heptad,* meaning a seven, and may be applied to whatever subject is under consideration. On the chart I have used the word *heptad,* which is the equivalent, in order to avoid confusion of terms.

It is also important to notice that these seventy sevens or four hundred ninety years are cut off from the entire period of time for Daniel's people, the Jews, and his holy city, Jerusalem. Therefore, the seventy weeks are *only running on while there is a remnant in Jerusalem owned of God as His people.*

And this brings me to a third point, which many have not noticed, that the cycle of the seventy weeks is divided into three parts. This you can see clearly by referring to the chart. First we have seven sevens, or forty-nine years. This is the period called the strait, or narrow, times in which the city and the walls of Jerusalem were rebuilt. The second part of the cycle consists of sixty-two weeks, or 434 years, after which Messiah was to be cut off and have nothing. This leaves one week, or seven years, yet to be fulfilled, and which never can be fulfilled until there is again a remnant of Judah in the city of Jerusalem owned by God as His people.

A cycle of 490 years had closed in the Babylonish captivity. Now, God said He was about to give them another period of the same length, at the end of which things would come out differently. Notice how much was to be accomplished before this period would close. Their transgression would be finished; an end made of sins; reconciliation, or properly, atonement, would be made for iniquity; everlasting righteousness—that is, the millennial kingdom—brought in; vision and prophecy all sealed up because fulfilled; and the Holy of Holies anointed in the future temple at Jerusalem.

Now it is very evident that there is a great deal here which has never yet been accomplished. Consequently, the 490 years have not yet been completed.

But can we tell definitely when the seventy weeks began? Yes, look at the twenty-fifth verse: "Know therefore and understand, that from the going forth of the commandment to restore and to build Jerusalem unto the Messiah the Prince shall be seven weeks, and threescore and two weeks." Now the going forth of the commandment to restore and build Jerusalem is given us in the second chapter of the book of Nehemiah, and there can be no question about the dates. The edict was given in the month Nisan, in the twentieth year of Artaxerxes the king, a year well known to historians as 445 B.C. Observe the commandment that went forth in the days of Cyrus, of which we have a record in Ezra 1, is clearly not the starting point referred to here. For that edict had to do alone with the rebuilding of the house of God at Jerusalem, that is, the temple of Zerubbabel. There is nothing said there about rebuilding the city or the wall. It is therefore the order of Artaxerxes that the angel here mentions as the true starting point.

Now from the time of this decree to the coming of Messiah the Prince, seven weeks, and sixty-two weeks, were to elapse, making in all sixty-nine weeks, or 483 years. The forty-nine years are distinguished from the rest because in them the city and the wall were rebuilt, and also, I doubt not, that our attention might be directed to the fact that the 490 years are divided into three series and do not necessarily run on in direct chronological order. It is true that the sixty-two weeks immediately followed the completion of the seven weeks. But this does not alter the fact that God distinctly separates the sixty-two weeks from the seven that went before, just as the last week, or seven years, is separated from all that preceded. Now able chronologists have shown that the crucifixion of the Lord Jesus Christ occurred immediately after the expiration of 483 prophetic years, of 360 days each, from the time of Artaxerxes' order. By reference to the other time-prophecies of this book it will become evident at once, I think, that this is the true method of computation. The time, times, and the dividing of time of 7:25 and 12:7 (representing exactly three-and-a-half years, as is evident by a comparison with the seven times in which Nebuchadnezzar was driven forth from among men) are clearly identical with the 1,260 days of the Apocalypse.

At the expiration of the sixty-nine weeks, therefore, the Messiah for whom

Israel had waited so long had actually come, only to be cut off and rejected by the very people who should have hailed His advent with joy. Up to this time, the great prophetic clock had been ticking out the years one after another in fulfillment of what we have in this chapter. But upon the crucifixion of the Lord Jesus Christ the great clock stopped, and there has not been another tick from it since, nor will there be until, in a coming day, the Jews shall be restored to their own land and a remnant be found among them who are ready to own the claims of God's Christ. Because of Jerusalem's rejection of her Prince, He has rejected them. He prophesied, before He died, that their city and temple would be thrown down and not one stone left upon another. This is also foretold in the twenty-sixth verse of our chapter: "The people of the prince that shall come shall destroy the city and the sanctuary; and the end thereof shall be with a flood, and unto the end [shall be war and desolations as] determined." These words briefly describe the history of Palestine from the coming of the Roman armies under Titus to the present time. Jerusalem, and Palestine as a whole, have been trodden down of all nations and shall be "until the times of the Gentiles be fulfilled" (Luke 21:24).

Observe that it is not said in verse twenty-six that the prince shall come at that time. In fact, it is distinctly stated that the city shall be destroyed not by the coming prince, but by his people. The prince is that dreadful character yet to arrive upon the scene, who will arrogate to himself supreme power in the days of the ten-kingdom period of the Roman Empire, which we have seen is still future. In other words, he is emphatically the Beast of Revelation 13:1 and 17:3.

He is the one who at once comes to the front in verse 27. *He* shall confirm a covenant with the many for one week. The seventieth week will begin when the Jewish people are restored in unbelief to their land and city, and among them will be found a faithful remnant, owning their sin and seeking Jehovah's face. The many, that is, the apostate mass of the people, will enter into covenant relations with the prince whose people formerly were the instruments of the destruction of their city. That is, this great blasphemous Roman leader will guarantee protection and freedom of religious worship to them for seven years, in return for which they will promise allegiance to him as their sovereign. In the midst of the week (that is, after three-and-a-half years), he will violate his part of the covenant and cause the sacrifices and oblations to Jehovah to cease. Idolatry of the most dreadful kind will be forced upon them. The direct result of which will be to distinguish the remnant from the mass, and thus to bring in the Great Tribulation that will continue for forty-two months—"a time, times, and half a time," or 1,260 days.

The last clause we may read either as we have it in the Authorized Version of our Bible as "that determined shall be poured upon the desolate" (v. 27), or, as others read it, "the desolator." That which God has determined shall be poured out upon poor desolate Judah because of their rejection of their rightful King and Savior. Then, when their cup has been filled to the brim by the dreadful persecutions of the Beast and Antichrist, these arch-enemies of God and His people shall themselves be punished with everlasting destruction from the presence of the Lord and the glory of His power. We have their doom clearly foretold in Revelation 19:20: "And the beast was taken, and with him the false prophet that wrought miracles before him, with which he deceived them that had received the mark of the beast, and them that worshipped his image. These both were cast alive into a lake of fire burning with brimstone." There they are seen a thousand years later, in 20:10, when the Devil, the instigator of all iniquity, shall be himself cast into the same fiery pit, "where the beast and the false prophet are, and shall be tormented day and night for ever and ever."

It is plain then, from all that we have been going over, that this last week of the seventy has not yet been fulfilled. For if it had been, the Jews would now be in their land, a holy, happy people, their temple anointed for divine service, their transgressions finished, and the years of their mourning ended. But God only counts time with Israel while they are owned as His people in the land of Palestine. All the years of their subjection to Gentile rule are looked upon as wasted. In this present age of their rejection, God is taking out from among the Gentiles a people to the name of the Lord Jesus—the church which will be His body and His bride for all eternity. When this great work is over, He "will build again the tabernacle of David, which is fallen down" (Acts 15:16), and commence once more to fulfill Old Testament prophecy from the point reached at the cross of Christ. Meantime, the Gentile oppressor stalks haughtily through the land of Palestine, and the poor Jew is despised and hated in most of the lands of his wanderings. The Lord Jesus gives us the history of Palestine in one pregnant sentence when He says, "[There shall be] wars and rumours of wars: . . . but the end is not yet" (Matt. 24:6). This is characteristic of the entire dispensation and shall be until the end. When will that end be? When the seventieth week begins to run, and God once more takes up the nation of Israel and begins to fulfill the promises made through the prophets, He will touch the pendulum of that great prophetic clock, as it were, and set it once more ticking off the years preparatory to ushering in the glorious kingdom of the Son of Man, when Jerusalem shall become the capital city of the world and Palestine be again the garden of the Lord.

Before closing, I briefly notice a rather peculiar interpretation that is frequently given to verse 27. It is said that the Lord Jesus is Himself to be "the prince that shall come" who confirms the covenant for one week. His own crucifixion is supposed to be the event which caused the sacrifice and oblation to cease. But neither chronologically nor doctrinally will this stand for a moment, if examined in the light of other Scripture passages. With whom did the Lord Jesus ever confirm a covenant for seven years? His precious blood is called "the blood of the everlasting covenant" (Heb. 13:20), not a covenant for one week of years. We may rest assured it is not Messiah at all, but the blasphemous prince who is yet to come who will fulfill what is predicted in this verse.

How near this world may be to the actual entering upon all these things no man can say, but it is the part of wisdom to learn from the prophetic Scripture passages and to turn now to Him who alone can save, to own Him as Redeemer and Lord, and thus be certain of being caught up to meet Him when He comes in the clouds before the time comes for His righteous judgment to be poured out upon this poor world.

LECTURE 10

ANGELIC AGENCY

Daniel 10

The last great prophecy, or revelation, made known to Daniel is set before us in detail in chapters 10–12. It is the most minute of all the prophecies given in the book. It commences with Daniel's day and culminates in the ushering in of the kingdom.

It is of importance to notice that here, as elsewhere in the prophetic Scripture passages, it is distinctively Daniel's people who are in view (see v. 14). We shall find nothing here, nor, for that matter, elsewhere in the Old Testament about the church of the present dispensation. It is because of lack of intelligence as to this that so much confusion has come in in the interpretation of prophecy.

We see from the opening verse of the book of Ezra, and from verse 1 of our chapter, that two years had elapsed between the time that king Cyrus gave permission to the Jews to return to Jerusalem and the time that Daniel had this vision. He himself was not one of those who returned, doubtless from the fact that he was in a position requiring his attendance upon the king and was also a very aged man, probably about ninety years old. We see him waiting quietly for the time when he is to leave the world behind in which he has seen so many changes and upheavals, but his heart is exercised about the remnant of his nation who have gone up to the place of Jehovah's name. You find him in deep grief, deep sorrow of heart—that sorrow of heart which perhaps only those know who, as Daniel, enter into the true state of the people of God. Even those who had gone up to Jerusalem failed from the very beginning in carrying out the mind of God in its fullness. They went up with a measure of enthusiasm and were gathered back to their holy city in ruin. But, alas, slothfulness and indifference to God's glory soon began to eat like a canker among them, and alliances were formed with the strangers surrounding Jerusalem, so that God really got very little out of their returning to the place of His temple and altar.

No doubt Daniel knew and felt all this, and his heart was grieved over it. He knew too that those who went up were very few indeed in comparison with those who remained at ease in the land where their bondage had given place to indifferent toleration. While they, as we see them in the book of Esther, seem quite content with the measure of liberty they enjoy and have apparently no heart for that which had so large a place in the mind of Daniel, he is found bowed before God in deep grief, mourning three full weeks. (And here I would have you notice the marginal reading, "weeks of *days*," bearing out that to which I called your attention in the last lecture, in regard to the use of the word *week*.) During this time of his mourning, he tasted no pleasant bread, nor flesh, nor wine, neither anointing himself at all, until the three whole weeks were fulfilled.

At the end of that time, as he was by the great river Hiddekel, in looking up he saw a certain man clothed in linen whose loins were girded with fine gold. His body is described as being like the beryl, his face as the appearance of lightning, and his eyes as lamps of fire. His arms and his feet were like polished brass, and the voice of his words like the voice of a multitude. The description cannot but recall to our minds that of the glorified Lord Himself as given in the first chapter of Revelation. But that this messenger who appeared to Daniel was not really a theophany, but a created angel, seems evident from the fact that he required the help of Michael in his conflict.[1] When Daniel beheld him, the men who were with him fled to hide themselves, though they saw not the vision, but a great quaking fell upon them. Left alone in the presence of this majestic being, the prophet's strength was turned into weakness and his vigor into corruption, so that he was upon the ground as one in a deep sleep, yet hearing the voice of the angel. A hand was stretched forth that touched him and set him upon his knees, though he was still obliged to support himself with the palms of his hands. Then the messenger spoke, saying, "O Daniel, a man greatly beloved, understand the words that I speak unto thee, and stand upright: for unto thee am I now sent" (v. 11). At this the prophet stood up trembling.

The angel then said, "Fear not, Daniel: for from the first day that thou didst set thine heart to understand, and to chasten thyself before thy God, thy words were heard, and I am come for thy words. But the prince of the kingdom of Persia withstood me one and twenty days: but, lo, Michael, one of the chief princes, came to help me; and I remained there with the kings of Persia" (vv. 12–13).

We get a remarkable insight here into the unseen world and the conflict even now being carried on in heavenly places. And may we not find here also the reason why many of our prayers do not seem to be answered when and as we would desire to have them? For three whole weeks Daniel had been before God in earnest supplication. He prayed, he besought, he interceded on behalf of his people, yet no answer had come. Had Daniel ceased praying, he might have given up the object of his prayers and declared that God turned a deaf ear to his petitions. But the angel tells him that at the very beginning of his supplication the commandment went forth, and he was sent from the very throne of God to make known to Daniel that which would set his mind at rest in regard to God's purpose and the final blessing of His people. But for twenty-one days this angel had been fighting his way through the fiends of the upper air. The prince of the kingdom of Persia (not Cyrus himself, but an evil angel evidently, delegated by Satan to seek to influence the hearts of the Persian kings against the people of God) had withstood this holy angel of the Lord for twenty-one days. Nor could the divinely sent messenger prevail until Michael, here called "one of the chief princes" and in the New Testament "the archangel," came to help him.

Now I grant you that all this is very mysterious. It is something altogether outside of the sphere of human cognizance. We know nothing whatsoever about the conflicts continuously being carried on in the unseen world, save what we can learn from our Bibles. But this much is clear: here was a man who was praying earnestly on earth, and God had heard that prayer in heaven. In answer to it He sent an angel, but for three weeks there was some hindrance keeping that angel from reaching Daniel. That hindrance was in the unseen world and by such a power that the archangel himself was needed to overcome it.

Now I would like to bring a few other Scriptures to your attention that have to do with this solemn subject. In the first chapters of the book of Job we find the sons of God presenting themselves before the Lord, and we are told that Satan came also. The sons of God are clearly an order of angelic ministers engaged in carrying out the will of God in connection with this world, in accordance with the word, "He . . . maketh his angels spirits, and his ministers a flame of fire. . . . Are they not all ministering spirits, sent forth to minister for them who shall be heirs of salvation?" (Heb. 1:7, 14). Among these sons of God, Satan, the foul leader of the evil hosts, walks unabashed. He acts—shall I say?—as one who has no fear of rebuke in that company. He is there, as on other occasions in Scripture, as the great adversary and accuser of the brethren. He accuses Job to the very face of God, and, as in the case of the apostle Peter and the other disciples, he seems to demand them that he may sift them as wheat. And the Lord does not deny his demand but delivers Job into his hands—for Job's own good, as we know. So we gather from this Scripture that God is able to use even the Devil to carry out His own purposes for the blessing of His children. He has not been outwitted by Satan, but uses him all through this present time. The Devil is the sifter of God's wheat. The Lord wants His wheat sifted; He does not want a lot of chaff. But when the Devil is thus used to sift God's wheat, when His children are thus put into the Devil's sieve, not one grain of the wheat is lost. The Devil is simply used by God for the separation of the chaff from the wheat—that is all. Do not despair then if, like Job and like Peter, you are put into the Devil's sieve. It is God Himself who is letting you be sifted like that, because He has seen the chaff in your life and wants the real to be separated from the false. But the point I had in mind in directing your attention to this Scripture was that all might see that good and evil angels alike have direct access to the presence of God.

In the eighteenth chapter of the book of 2 Chronicles we have the account of an alliance entered into by Ahab and Jehoshaphat. Ahab was a wicked king, the ruler of the ten tribes. Jehoshaphat was in large measure a man of God, but unhappily he was a man who could not say "No." He was of too yielding a character for his own good and the good of the kingdom of Judah over which he ruled. At Ahab's request, he had promised to go out to battle to help him against his enemies, but Jehoshaphat desired also to consult a prophet of the Lord. Ahab brought in a host of the prophets of Baal, who all predicted a glorious victory. But this did not satisfy Jehoshaphat, and so Micaiah, a prophet of Jehovah imprisoned for his faithfulness, is brought from his dungeon to declare the mind of the Lord. When he came, the king of Israel said, "Shall we go . . . to battle?" And Micaiah replied, ironically, Oh yes, "Go ye up, and prosper, and they shall be delivered into your hand" (2 Chron. 18:14). But the king detected the tone of irony in his voice, and Ahab adjured him to tell him the truth. At that, Micaiah drew aside, as it were, the veil from the other world and declared that he had seen a multitude of spirits surrounding the throne of God. One of these, in obedience to the divine permission, had been sent forth to become a lying spirit in the mouth of Ahab's prophets that he might seduce the wretched idolatrous king to his destruction. Here again we see the same thing that is brought before us in the book of Job—angels, both good and evil, having access to heaven.

It is the same in the third chapter of Zechariah. What a beautiful picture we have there! Joshua, the high priest, is the representative of the whole nation of Israel. He stands before the Lord clothed in filthy garments—a picture of one chosen of God and yet defiled by sin. An adversary is there to accuse him, but the angel of Jehovah is standing by. Who is that mystic angel of Jehovah? Who but He of whom Jehovah said, "My name is in Him" (Exod. 23:21)? He speaks to us of the Lord Jesus Himself, the Messenger of the covenant. What does Jehovah say when Satan attempts to accuse? "The LORD rebuke thee, O Satan; . . . is not this a brand plucked out of the fire?" (Zech. 3:2). This brings out two things: first, there is God's sovereign electing grace, and second, then, there is redemption. That is why God could recognize and own the remnant of Israel in spite of their failures. Jehovah says, "I have chosen him"—that is His answer to Satan. For "the gifts and calling of God are without repentance" (Rom. 11:29). But this is based upon redemption, for He says unto those who stood by, "Take away the filthy garments from him. And unto him he said, Behold, I have caused thine iniquity to pass from thee, and I will clothe thee with change of raiment" (Zech. 3:4). The presence of the Angel of the covenant points on to the *Cross*. For it was at that cross the covenant would be ratified in His precious blood who became Man with the view to the suffering of death, that He might cleanse from all iniquity those whom He redeemed to Himself. Thus we have full redemption and the brand plucked out of the fire.

Now let us link up with this that important passage in Revelation 12. Remember that it speaks of something that is still future.

> There was war in heaven: Michael and his angels fought against the dragon; and the dragon fought and his angels, and prevailed not; neither was their place found any more in heaven. And the great dragon was cast out, that old serpent, called the Devil, and Satan, which deceiveth the whole world: he was cast out into the earth, and his angels were cast out with him. And I heard a loud voice saying in heaven, Now is come salvation, and strength, and the kingdom of our God, and the power of his Christ: for the accuser of our brethren is cast [out], which accused them before our God day and night. (vv. 7–10)

This gives us the end of Satan's place as the accuser with access to the heavens. He is driven forth by that same Michael who came to the assistance of the angel who speaks to Daniel in our chapter. This event will take place in the midst of the seventieth week of the ninth chapter, and after that no foul spirit will ever more have access to the presence of God.

In the sixth chapter of the epistle to the Ephesians there is a passage of great importance. See verses 11–12: "Put on the whole armour of God, that ye may be able to stand against the wiles of the devil. For we wrestle not against flesh and blood, but against principalities, against powers, against the world rulers of the darkness, against wicked spirits in heavenly places" (literal translation). The Christian's foes are these wicked spirits, who, like the prince of the kingdom of Persia, are ruling the hearts of men in these days of darkness. Against their wiles we are warned. The great business of Satan at the present time is to seek to deceive the people of God with things that seem to be in accordance with His mind, but which are really deceitful imitations.

You remember, when Joshua and the people of Israel entered the land of Canaan, God told them to utterly destroy all the nations that dwelt in it. But the Gibeonites, filled with terror, sent an ambassage to Joshua pretending to have come from a long distance, and by means of their moldy bread, ragged clothes, and worn shoes, deceived the leaders of Israel into entering into a league with them. Thus they were misled by not being on their guard against the wiles of the Canaanites. And we, too, will be deceived by the hellish stratagems of our great adversary if we be not careful to continuously ask counsel of the Lord. In this sixth chapter of Ephesians we are told that our warfare is with "the world rulers of this darkness." Who are these world rulers? They are not the king of England, the emperor of Germany, the czar of Russia, or the president of this great republic. These great and often good men have to do with the temporal government of this world. They are "the powers that be," ordained of God. Yet they may be like the little figures on the chessboard, in the hands of the real world rulers of this darkness.[2]

This is what we learn in this tenth chapter of Daniel. The prince of the kingdom of Persia who withstood the angel of the Lord twenty-one days was one of the world rulers of this darkness. The prince of Grecia of verse 20 was another one seeking to influence the hearts of the Grecian rulers against the will of God. And then, on the other hand, have you noticed what Michael is called in the last verse? He is designated as "Michael *your* prince," and in 12:1 he is called "the great prince which standeth for the children of *thy* people." That is, Michael the archangel seems in a special manner to have a care for the people of Israel. Thus, while evil angels were seeking Israel's ruin, Michael and his hosts of benevolent angels were protecting their interests.

You will remember how efforts were being made at this very time to thwart God's purposes concerning the Jews. Sanballat and his companions sought in every way they could to hinder the progress of the work of the Lord at Jerusalem.

What was going on upon the earth was evidently intimately connected with, in fact the result of, what was going on in the upper air. Satan is called the prince of the power of the air, and his angelic subordinates and God's holy angels were warring in connection with the attempt to carry out that which God Himself had planned for His earthly people.

Perhaps the chief of all the world rulers of this darkness is described in Ezekiel 28:11–18. You will notice that in the first ten verses of the chapter the prince of Tyre is spoken of, but from verse 11 on we have a very different being, one who is clearly superhuman, designated as the king of Tyre. Of him Ezekiel says,

> Thus saith the Lord GOD; Thou sealest up the sum, full of wisdom, and perfect in beauty. Thou hast been in Eden the garden of God; every precious stone was thy covering, the sardius, topaz, and the diamond, the beryl, the onyx, and the jasper, the sapphire, the emerald, and the carbuncle, and gold: the workmanship of thy tabrets and of thy pipes was prepared in thee in the day that thou wast created. Thou art the anointed cherub that covereth; and I have set thee so: thou wast upon the holy mountain of God; thou hast walked up and down in the midst of the stones of fire. Thou wast perfect in thy ways from the day that thou wast created, till iniquity was found in thee. By the multitude of thy merchandise they have filled the midst of thee with violence, and thou hast sinned: therefore I will cast thee as profane out of the mountain of God: and I will destroy thee, O covering cherub, from the midst of the stones of fire. Thine heart was lifted up because of thy beauty, thou hast corrupted thy wisdom by reason of thy brightness: I will cast thee to the ground, I will lay thee before kings, that they may behold thee. (Ezekiel 28:12–17)

Was all this true of any earthly king of Tyre? Surely not. But it was true of the great prince, the unseen ruler, who was leading on the kingdom of Tyre to its doom. Alas, how readily do rulers and nations obey the behests of these malignant spirits, who, having lost heaven for themselves, now seem to find their delight in encompassing the ruin of mankind! And though God in His grace is seeking man's blessing, and has given His Word and Spirit to guide in paths of righteousness and peace, as well as having sent forth hosts of unfallen elect angels to influence leaders and led to prefer justice and holiness to unrighteousness and iniquity, yet so perverse is the heart of man that in his natural state he is ever ready to be led by the Devil captive at his will.

In the present age our conflict as Christians is said to be with *principalities* and *powers* who are not of flesh and blood. This makes it evident that there are degrees in rank among angels, whether fallen or unfallen, as there are in human armies. The special effort of these organized hosts of hell is now to deceive the people of God by presenting something else for their hearts to take the place of Christ and His truth and, thus, keep them out of their blessing. Coupled with this is the effort to hinder exercised souls from coming to the knowledge of the truth at all by imitating that which is of God, that those may be turned aside into the devious mazes of error who would otherwise seem about to obey the truth.

Have you noticed how every precious truth of Scripture has its satanic counterfeit? It has been so from the very beginning. Scarcely was the glorious gospel of grace proclaimed when the Devil introduced men secretly among the assemblies of God, whose object was to turn that very grace into lasciviousness. If the apostle taught that the Christian was not under law, but grace, then the antinomian was almost at his heels to cry, "Let us do evil, that good may come." And it is the same in our day. Let the precious truth of the indwelling and gifts of the Holy Spirit be declared, and Satan will follow with false gifts and another spirit, leading even earnest souls into the wildest fanaticism. Let the truth of new birth be insisted upon, and the Devil will wise up teachers after his own heart to tell men that being born again means simply "rising out of the self-life into the spiritual, reaching out after the higher ideals, seeking to make that which is highest, noblest and best of ourselves; thus saving ourselves by character."[3] This is a sample of the teaching heard in many a supposedly orthodox pulpit at the present time.

Again, let one begin to preach that the Lord Jesus Christ is coming again, let him put forth the blessed truth of the rapture of the church at the Lord's return, and you will have the wicked spirits in heavenly places poisoning men's minds with so many unscriptural and false conceptions about this solemn and important theme that the second advent becomes a byword in the minds of some intelligent people—they become sick and tired of the whole thing. But these are just the wiles of the Devil against which the believer is warned, and concerning which we need to be on our guard, remembering the word, "Prove all things; hold fast that which is good" (1 Thess. 5:21).

Thank God, the hosts of the upper air are not all malevolent. You remember at the siege of Dothan, in answer to the prayer of Elisha, the Lord opened the eyes of the prophet's servant, and he saw the mountains round about full of fiery chariots. "The angel of the LORD encampeth round about them that fear him"

(Ps. 34:7). O beloved, we too need opened eyes! Then we would see the angelic host camping around us for our protection and watching over us for good. Thus we would fight on with new courage, clad in the whole armor of God, knowing that against Christ's church, founded upon Himself, the gates of hell shall not prevail.

And now, in closing this solemn subject, let me say a word to the unsaved. These wicked spirits of which I have been speaking are determined upon your soul's damnation. They will use every effort known to fiends to hinder your salvation and to seal your doom. How much, then, you need to learn the lesson that in yourself you have no strength or power. You are but a poor, weak, easily-deceived soul led by Satan and imposed upon by his wicked hosts. One alone can deliver you from your dreadful foes. That One is the blessed Lord Jesus Christ who died upon the cross "that through death he might destroy [render powerless or annul] him that had the power of death, that is, the devil; and deliver them who through fear of death were all their lifetime subject to bondage" (Heb. 2:14–15). Call, then, upon Him and be delivered from the tearful and superhuman enemies who desire your eternal ruin, for it is written that "Whosoever shall call upon the name of the Lord shall be saved" (Rom. 10:13).

Let us now, after this long parenthesis, turn back to our chapter. In verse 14, the angel tells Daniel that he had come to make him understand what should befall the prophet's people, the Jews, in the latter days. At this, Daniel set his face toward the ground and became dumb. Another angel then drew near and touched his lips, at which he spoke aloud and said unto the glorious being who stood before him, "O my lord, by the vision my sorrows are turned upon me, and I have retained no strength. For how can the servant of this my lord talk with this my lord? for as for me, straightway there remained no strength in me, neither is there breath left in me" (vv. 16–17). The ministering angel touched him again, strengthening him and bidding him fear not but be strong. At this, Daniel bade the revealing angel speak on. He tells him that he must return to fight with the prince of Persia and that when he has gone forth the prince of Grecia shall come. But first he is commissioned to show Daniel "that which is noted in the scripture of truth" (v. 21). This is clearly a record kept not on earth but in heaven, the omniscient God having outlined, long before it comes to pass on earth, the events to occur in the kingdoms of men. This revelation is given us in the next chapter.

As "in the roll of the book" it was written of the eternal Son of God, "I delight to do thy will, O my God: yea, thy law is within my heart" (Ps. 40:8). Just as every step of His journey from the throne of the universe down to the cross of

Calvary and back to the throne, yes, on to the ages of ages, was foreknown from before the foundation of the world, so has God foreseen all that is to transpire upon this planet in the affairs of men. In the "scripture of truth" recorded above, all is ever before His eyes. Let Satan and evil men rage as they will, He "worketh all things after the counsel of his own will" (Eph. 1:11).

The Christian heart may surely rest in this, rejoicing in this knowledge, that, at all times,

> God sits as sovereign on His throne,
> And ruleth all things well!

THE WARS OF THE PTOLEMIES AND THE SELEUCIDS

Daniel 11:1–35

In taking up the first part of this chapter, I want to impress upon you again the words of the apostle Paul, several times already alluded to in these lectures, that "all scripture is given by inspiration of God and is *profitable*" (2 Tim. 3:16). For in seeking to expand this particular portion, I shall be obliged to occupy you, almost entirely, with a running historical outline of events, covering a period of something like two hundred years, in connection with the wars that desolated the land of Palestine after the death of Alexander the Great. This may seem to some very dry and unspiritual, but the subject, if it is to be made at all lucid and plain, seems to me to demand the kind of treatment I purpose giving it. And I feel sure, if carefully noted, it will give many to see, as never before, the absolute unerring precision of God's Holy Word.

We have here set forth for our learning a record that was first made in heaven. It must be that God intended us to study it and to understand it, or He would not have included it in the volume of Scripture. And for this we must take some pains, for it is a portion of the Word that we cannot clearly understand unless we take the trouble to investigate a little and see how it has been fulfilled. Now if

105

there are those who decry the study of historical and other subjects in connection with the Word of God, I would remind such again of the pregnant sentence that "All history is His story." And surely the man of God can lose nothing but gain much by observing how remarkably history confirms prophecy and thus sets its seal upon the divine inspiration of the Bible. The Holy Spirit never condemns our acquiring the knowledge of this world. That which is set aside as untrustworthy, fruitful only of strife, speculation, and vain wrangling is the "wisdom" of this world. That is, we are warned against human philosophy, against the reasoning of the human mind uninstructed by and unopened to divine illumination. But we are not warned against the acquisition of true knowledge if we couple with it the fear of God and the love of the Spirit.

God does not put a premium upon ignorance. Some Christians are most shortsighted, narrowminded, and bigoted; intolerant of the opinions of others; or, in fact, of anything outside their own range of vision. Undoubtedly the best cure for this very unchristlike spirit is to be more in the company of the blessed Lord Himself; but to this may well be added a helpful, broadening knowledge of facts and events, especially in connection with Scripture.

The angel who had appeared to Daniel tells him that in the first year of Darius the Mede, after Babylon's overthrow, he had stood to strengthen him. In the second verse he begins, as it were, to unroll the scroll of the Scripture of truth. "Behold," he says, "there shall stand up yet three kings in Persia; and the fourth shall be far richer than they all: and by his strength through his riches he shall stir up all against the realm of Grecia" (v. 2). We saw in chapter ten that this vision was given to Daniel in the third year of Cyrus. The three kings who were to follow were first, his son Cambyses, who was succeeded not by his own son Smerdis but by a wretched impostor generally called Pseudo-Smerdis. He looked very much like the son of Cambyses, and by trickery had himself proclaimed emperor and reigned in the name of Smerdis. Darius Hystaspes succeeded him, and he, in his turn, was succeeded by Xerxes the Great. This Xerxes was not the last king of Persia, nor is it so stated here though at first sight it might seem to be implied. But he was the fourth and, as prophesied, "far richer than they all." He stirred up Asia against the realm of Grecia and, with an immense army of over two million and a half (if we can trust the computation of the historians of those days), crossed the Hellespont and invaded Greece. But the very size of his army defeated his own purpose, and his hosts were driven back into Asia. The Grecians never forgave this insult to their race and nursed the desire for vengeance until the days of Alexander the Great, who is the "mighty king" referred to in verse 3.

There is quite an interval between verses four and five, which is passed over in silence in order to connect the invasion of Alexander with the effort of Xerxes to conquer Greece. After Alexander had established his authority over all Greece, he determined to pass over into Asia with the special object of wiping out the disgrace referred to. He met the forces of Darius Codomanus, utterly defeated them, and laid hold of all the Persian dominion but passed away himself, very shortly afterward, in a drunken revel. He died in the very prime of his life, a wretched victim of ill living. Thus was fulfilled the word, "And when he shall stand up, his kingdom shall be broken" (v. 4). The verse goes on to tell us that it "shall be divided toward the four winds of heaven; and not to his posterity, nor according to his dominion which he ruled: for his kingdom shall be plucked up, even for others beside those." Now all this was fulfilled to the letter. Alexander had two sons, Hercules and Alexander, but both were slain—one before, and the other after his death. His kingdom was then divided, as God had said it should be. After the battle of Ipsus, which took place in B.C. 301, his dominions were parceled out, as we have already seen in chapters 7–8, among four of his generals. From this point on, our chapter occupies us only with the dominions and the doings of two of them and their successors, namely, Ptolemy Lagus, ruler of Egypt and Seleucas, Satrap of Syria. Thus the great world empire that Alexander had established at such a tremendous cost was broken into warring fragments, none of which ever again attained the splendor or power of his kingdom.

From verses 5–35 we have the wars of the Seleucids and the Ptolemies for about two centuries. These rulers are called, respectively, the king of the north and the king of the south—the directions having to do, of course, with the land of Palestine, which in God's eye is the center of the earth.

> When the Most High divided to the nations their inheritance, when He separated the sons of Adam, He set the bounds of the people according to the number of the children of Israel. For the LORD'S portion is His people; Jacob is the lot of his inheritance. (Deuteronomy 32:8–9)

The reason that the other two kingdoms do not here appear upon the page of prophecy is thus made clear. The angel told Daniel he was going to show him what should befall his people, and those two kingdoms had no place in connection with Israel or their land.

It will almost be necessary to take up what we are now to have before us verse by verse. I pray God that as we do so, it may impress every heart with the absolute perfection of the Holy Scriptures and their correctness down to the smallest detail. The king of the south mentioned in verse 5 was Ptolemy Lagus. The expression "one of his princes" may refer either to the fact that Ptolemy was one of Alexander's princes or, as others judge more likely, that Seleucas Nicator was, in the beginning, subject to Ptolemy, who was strong above him and had the greatest dominion of the four into which the empire had been divided. But upon the death of Lagus, when Ptolemy Soter succeeded him, conditions were reversed. The dominion of Seleucas was enlarged by the annexation of Babylon, Media, and the surrounding nations. He threw off his allegiance to Egypt and ruled independently. Naturally, this brought about a state of warfare and enmity between the two kingdoms, but as we read in verse 6, "In the end of years they shall join themselves together."

This was in the reign of Nicator's grandson, Antiochus Theos. In his days a treaty of peace was arranged with Ptolemy Philadelphus, which was confirmed by the king's daughter of the south, Berenice, being given in marriage to Antiochus, who divorced his own wife Laodice for this purpose. But God had declared that she "shall not retain the power of the arm; neither shall he stand, nor his arm: but she shall be given up, and they that brought her, and he that begat her, and he that strengthened her in these times" (v. 6). All this was fulfilled as predicted. Laodice managed to stir up her friends against the king, and, as a result, Berenice and all her attendants were put to death. Antiochus then reinstated his divorced queen, who shortly afterward poisoned him and had her son Seleucas Callinicus crowned in his stead.

"Out of a branch of the roots" of Berenice, that is from her family, one was to stand up in his place for office and come with an army into the fortress of the king of the north, and prevail against him (v. 7). This refers to her brother, Ptolemy Euergetes, who with a mighty army forced his way across the land of Palestine, spreading desolation everywhere, actuated by the desire to avenge the murder of his sister and to wipe out the dishonor inflicted on Egypt. He was everywhere successful, utterly defeating Callinicus and reaping an immense spoil. But tidings of a sedition in Egypt caused him to hasten back, carrying with him an immense number of captives with 'their gods, with their princes, and with their precious vessels of silver and of gold." He did not return to Syria, and Callinicus himself died shortly afterward by a fall from his horse. Ptolemy reigned four years longer, thus continuing "more years than the king of the north" (v. 8).

In the tenth verse the sons of Callinicus are contemplated. These are known in history as Seleucus Ceraunus and Antiochus the Great. They assembled a great force to inflict retribution upon the Egyptians. But Ceraunus died in less than two years, leaving his brother sole ruler. He was one of the most notable kings of those days and lost no time in pressing an Egyptian invasion. He led an army of seventy-five thousand against the hereditary foes of his house. But he proved no match for the indolent and despised king of the south, Ptolemy Philopator, who could barely be dragged away from his pleasures and follies to lead an army against the invaders. At the Battle of Eaphia, he defeated Antiochus with great slaughter, reconquered all that had been wrested from him, put Antiochus under tribute, and returned to Egypt crowned with military glory. But like another Alexander, he then gave himself up to out-and-out wickedness and licentiousness, and, upon a revolt soon after occurring in Syria, concluded an ignoble peace with Antiochus because he was too depraved and indolent to follow up his victories. Upon his death, Egypt sank lower than it had been for years. All this we have briefly sketched in verses 11–12.

Upon the succession of his son Ptolemy Epiphanes, a mere child, to the throne, Antiochus the Great formed an alliance with Philip the Third of Macedon and sought also to rally the Jews to his standard. The faithful among them refused to serve in his army, but the apostates, called in verse 14 "the robbers of thy people," readily entered into covenant with him and proved a very great help on a number of occasions. With his united armies he besieged the Egyptian garrison left in Jerusalem and put it to the sword. He defeated Scopias, the Egyptian general at Paneas, who fled to Sidon, a fenced city, but was there destroyed. The Egyptian armies, sent for the deliverance of Paneas, were likewise routed, and Antiochus found himself everywhere supreme. Upon his return from the Egyptian wars, he entered into "the glorious land," that is, Palestine, where, because of the help rendered by his Jewish troops, he bestowed upon the people many evidences of his favor. The last clause of verse 16 should read, "which by his hand shall be perfected." It refers undoubtedly to the fact that in his time Palestine became a more peaceful and fruitful country than it had been for half a century.

Verse 17 was fulfilled in his effort to undermine the remaining influence and power of Ptolemy Epiphanes by giving him his daughter Cleopatra to wife, having previously charged her that she should, after her marriage, in everything act for her father's interests. But it was written, "she shall not stand on his side, neither be for him" (v. 17). Cleopatra proved a faithful wife to Epiphanes, supporting him against her father, who was naturally much disappointed that his well-laid plans had completely miscarried.

He determined now to extend the glory of his dominions by conquering Greece. The isles of the Aegean Sea were first subjugated to his sway, and he then crossed over with his armies into Greece. But now a most unlooked-for event took place. The Iron Kingdom, destined to be the fourth and last upon earth before the establishment of the kingdom of the Son of Man, was at this time just beginning to make its presence felt. The Grecians had entered into an alliance—offensive and defensive—with the Romans, and so they at once notified their powerful allies of the danger to which they were exposed. The senate commissioned Lucius Scipio Asiaticus to go to their relief with an army of tried warriors. He met Antiochus in battle and utterly defeated him, and on the most ignominious terms sent him back to his home. Scipio is undoubtedly the prince or, as some render it, captain referred to in verse 18. Thus Antiochus, humbled and in deep distress, turned his face toward "the fort of his own land" (v. 19). But, according to the writing of the Scripture of truth, he was to stumble and fall and not be found. This he did, for in his need and desperation, attempting with a band of soldiers to plunder the temple of Jupiter at Elymais, he and his warriors were slain by the infuriated populace, incensed at what they considered an act of sacrilege of the gravest nature.

In verse 20 we read, "Then shall stand up in his estate [one that causeth an exactor to pass over; margin], in the glory of the kingdom: but within few days he shall be destroyed, neither in anger, nor in battle." This was the son of Antiochus, Seleucus Philopator, who, in desperate need of money owing to the wretched condition in which his father had left the kingdom, sent Heliodorus to plunder the temple of Jehovah at Jerusalem. Upon his return with the booty, he treacherously assassinated his master after he had reigned twelve years, a "few days" in contrast to the long reign of Antiochus, which extended to nearly forty years.

THE Anti. Christ

From verse 21 to the end of verse 35, we have before us the fearful monster who has well been called the "Antichrist of the Old Testament," because of his unfailing enmity to the people and worship of Jehovah. He is the same as the one of whom we have already studied in the eighth chapter—the infamous and blasphemous "Little Horn" that sprang out of one of the four horns upon the head of the Grecian goat. His name is execrated to this day by all Jews in every land. He was called by his fawning courtiers Antiochus Epiphanes, that is, the splendid or magnificent. But some wag of his day changed one letter of his name and called him Antiochus Epimanes, that is, the mad man, because of his wild pranks and almost insane follies and brutalities. He was stirred with such hatred against the Jews and their religion that there was no atrocity too great for this wretched king to perpetrate. He is well described as a vile person, who came in peaceably, and obtained the kingdom by flatteries. At the beginning, he made a league both with the Jews and with Ptolemy Philometer but proved false to each, as God had declared he would (vv. 22–24). "The prince of the covenant" in Israel was, I judge, a title given here to the high priest. It is a notorious fact that Epiphanes degraded the office to the last degree, selling the high priesthood to the vilest man to be found among the apostate part of the people.

In accordance with verse 25, he stirred "up his power and his courage against the king of the south with a great army," and the king of the south, Philometer, came against him to battle "with a very great and mighty army." But he was unable to stand because of devices forecasted against him, namely, through the treachery of his own sons and household servants, who betrayed him to Antiochus, thus fulfilling verse 26: "Yea, they that feed of the portion of his meat shall destroy him, and his army shall overflow: and many shall fall down slain." Professing great magnanimity, Antiochus proposed a truce, and the two kings met "at one table." There they made promises which they never intended to keep, thus "speaking lies" (v. 27).

Angered by the exultation of the Jews, who had heard that he had been slain in Egypt, Antiochus marched his armies against Jerusalem, which he caused to pass through all the horrors of a siege and sack, sparing neither age, sex, nor condition. In their desperation the Jews appealed to the Romans, who had before interfered on behalf of the Grecians, and requested their assistance in what was to them a life-and-death struggle for their religion and their liberty. Marching against the Maccabees, Antiochus was met by Popilius Loenus and the other Roman envoys at the head of an army. Popilius demanded that Antiochus at once cease his interference with the Jews and bind himself to accept the decree of the Roman senate, keep the peace, and acknowledge Rome's authority. Epiphanes asked for time to consider the terms proposed for his acceptance. But Popilius with his sword or staff at once drew a circle around Antiochus and demanded that he decide before he stepped out of the ring. Having no alternative, he submitted, evidently with no intention of keeping the pledges he made. The "ships of Chittim" of verse 30 refer doubtless to the Roman galleys sent in response to the pitiful plea of the Jews.

After the Romans had gone, Antiochus forswore his allegiance and turned once more upon the devoted sons of Israel, "[having] indignation against the holy covenant." Certain traitorous Jews, here described as "them that forsake the holy covenant," formed a league with him and betrayed their own compatriots to the tyrant who hated them. He set up a statue of Jupiter Olympus, whom he identified with himself, in the temple at Jerusalem, sacrificed a sow upon the altar, and put a stop to the oblations to Jehovah, declaring that he alone should be an object of worship. The faithful of Judah, horrified beyond measure at his unspeakable sacrilege, led by the heroic family of the Maccabees, took up arms against him and were slaughtered by thousands. This was the placing of "the abomination that maketh desolate," predicted in verse 31, in connection with the pollution of the sanctuary and the taking away of the daily sacrifice.

The next chapter speaks of another abomination of desolation, which our Lord Jesus Christ in Matthew 24 declared was still future when He was on earth. Of that abomination we shall read in the last chapter. The twenty-three hundred days of chapter 8 commenced with this act of desecration by Antiochus. At the end of that period, the sanctuary was cleansed and sacrifices to Jehovah reinstituted.

Verses 32–35 describe the conditions prevailing among the Jews in that awful time of suffering, never to be paralleled until the Great Tribulation of the last days. In fact, they picture the whole history of the people of Judah from the time when they were joined to the Roman Empire right on to the time of the end, or the seventieth week of which we have already spoken.

Between verses 35 and 36 there is an interval of many centuries. The history of the kings of the north and south is now closed, and another dreadful character, of whom Antiochus Epiphanes was merely a forerunner or type, is at once introduced—the willful king, the great personal Antichrist of the last days. Of him our next lecture will treat.

And now, in concluding this historical outline of the wars of the kings of the north and the south, I would press upon each one that prophecy is indeed but history prewritten. And, in this instance, even in the minutest details, history is seen to be prophecy fulfilled. Terrible indeed is the presumption of any, who with such a record in their hands refuse to heed its solemn lessons and deliberately reject the testimony of the inspired Word of God. It seems to me that even the natural mind, if at all unbiased and willing to learn, must be impressed by this remarkable correspondence between history and prophecy, leading any truly honest soul to exclaim, "God spake all these words" (Exod. 20:1).

And remember that He who spoke *these* words is the God who has inspired all Scripture, and who will hold all men responsible to accept the testimony He gives them, upon pain of everlasting banishment from His holy presence if they persist in rebelling against His authority and refusing His Word. That Word is given you now to warn you of your danger and point the way to salvation. That Word will be opened on the day of judgment, and if you appear there unsaved, you must be judged according to what is there written. And just as in the ages to come when the redeemed look back over their pathway here on earth, they shall exclaim like Israel in the land of Canaan, "There hath not failed one word of all his good promise" (1 Kings 8:56), so will each lost soul cry out in bitter anguish, "Not one word has failed of all that God declared in regard to the doom of the impenitent and the Christ rejecter!"

Oh, how important, then, that you have to do with the God who gave you the Bible, now, on the ground of the atoning work of His blessed Son, that you should know Him as your own personal Savior. Would that you might be aroused by these addresses—you who have no hope and are without God in the world—to see the danger in which you stand and your need of turning to Him, who once in infinite grace gave Himself for our sins on Calvary's cross of shame.

The Maccabees, in the days of Antiochus, were called the hammers of God, and God has asked, "Is not my word like a fire? . . . and like a hammer that breaketh the rock in pieces?" Preaching the gospel is just like hammering away at hard hearts. Alas, that there is so little response! I have heard of a gentleman, a traveling man, who used to go to a town where there were many great factories and foundries. In that town scores of immense steel hammers were pounding away continuously. The noise was deafening, and this gentleman of whom I speak found it impossible to sleep in that town, for there was no cessation of the noise day or night.

But the people of the town were so thoroughly used to it that they could sleep on through it all. But one night something went wrong with the power plant, and all the hammers stopped. At once all the town woke up. What awakened them? It was the unusual quiet and stillness succeeding the years of deafening sound. Beloved friends, the day has now drawn very near when God's hammers shall all cease their pounding. Soon gospel days will have ended; preaching the message of love and grace which you have refused so long will have ceased. Then, ah then! there will indeed be a great awakening—an awakening when it is too late to be saved. When the great men and the chief captains and the mighty men, and every bondman and every free man will hide themselves in the dens and in caves of the mountains and will cry to the rocks, "Fall on us; and to the hills, Cover us" (Luke 23:30), and, "Fall on us, and hide us from the face of him that sitteth on the throne, and from the wrath of the Lamb: for the great day of his wrath is come; and who shall be able to stand?" (Rev. 6:16).

But no hiding place will avail in that day, for God will then be dealing no longer in grace, but in stern intrinsic justice with those who have not received the love of the truth that they might be saved. Their heartrending cry will be, "The harvest is past, the summer is ended, and we are not saved" (Jer. 8:20).

O dear unsaved one, weigh these things well and trifle no longer with the question of the eternal destiny of your precious soul still unsettled. If you continue to do despite to the Spirit of grace, "What wilt thou say when he shall punish thee?" (Jer. 13:21).

THE ANTICHRIST

Daniel 11:36–45

"Ye have heard," says the apostle John, "that antichrist shall come" (1 John 2:18). He at once goes on to say that already there are many antichrists. But he distinguishes clearly between these lesser forerunners of the final apostasy and the future impious personage who is so frequently mentioned in prophecy as the very incarnation of lawlessness and blasphemy but is only here distinctly called by name.

I suppose there are very few prophetic teachers, of any scriptural discernment, who question the application of the present passage to Antichrist. The only question would be as to his identity, and as to that a great many different solutions of the problem have been proposed. According to many, Antiochus Epiphanes fulfilled in himself all that is here predicted of the willful king. Others, who recognize the interval referred to in the last address between verses 35 and 36, apply the passage, together with the first part of Revelation 13, which they consider parallel with this, to the emperor Nero, the first Roman persecutor of the Christians. To many of the fathers, Simon Magus, the impostor of Acts 8, was the Antichrist. Some Romanist doctors applied the passage to Muhammad, the false prophet of Arabia, while Protestant interpreters without number from Luther's day to the present have found in these words a description of the papacy. Others there are—and their judgment seems to me to be the correct one—who hold that neither any nor all of these characters fully meet the requirements of the case, and that consequently the Antichrist is still to arise in the future and will come upon the scene only in the time of the end.

Before concluding this lecture, I hope to make clear my reasons for not being able to accept the hypothesis that the papacy, while manifestly antichristian in character, is the Antichrist. At present I shall simply endeavor to bring out what seems to me to be the clear teaching of the passage.

And first, in order that we may have plainly before our minds the part to be played by Antichrist in the world's great crisis, I desire briefly to attempt to point out the various leaders who are to occupy prominent positions in the coming day.

We have already found, in our study of this book, that in the latter times, when the transgressors are come to the full, the Roman Empire is to be revived in a ten-kingdomed condition. Ten European powers are to be united in one federation. To bring this about, there will be a union of socialistic and imperialistic policies. One of these ten kings will become arbiter of Europe. This chief ruler it is who is called in Revelation 13:1–8 and other portions, emphatically, *"the* Beast." In the seventh chapter of Daniel he is seen as the Little Horn of the West. In the time of the end this Little Horn, the Beast, will have his seat in Rome. He will be utterly infidel, throwing off all pretension to the fear of God, and will set himself up as the only god worthy of adoration. To him apostate Christendom will pay universal homage after the destruction of the great antichurch, "Babylon, the mother of harlots and abominations of the earth." This worship will evidently not only be the acknowledgment that deity dwells in this man, it will be also the recognition of the blasphemous tenet (for which Christian Science, so-called, and the self-styled New Thought are now preparing the way) that God and man are one. The Beast will be the embodiment of intellectual force and brilliancy, the peerless coming man for whom the nations have been waiting so long. Like Napoleon Bonaparte, who perhaps more nearly corresponded to this character than any other man that ever lived, he will dazzle the nations by his almost superhuman abilities and unparalleled success. To him men will gladly grant the title Napoleon arrogated to himself, "The Man of Destiny."

In the East, as we saw in chapter eight, another power will for a time dispute the preeminence of the Beast. This will be the Little Horn of Asia. The last Gentile ruler of the lands now dominated by Turkey will be the one in whom this prophecy is fulfilled. He is in no sense to be confounded with the Little

Horn of the seventh chapter. The one arises out of the Roman Empire; the other, from one of the divisions of the empire of Alexander the Great. This latter king is identified, I believe, with the Assyrian of Isaiah 10:24–25. He will be the special enemy of the Jews in the time of the end. In the passage referred to we read after the prophecy of the return of the remnant to their land, "Therefore thus saith the Lord GOD of hosts, O my people that dwellest in Zion, be not afraid of the Assyrian: he shall smite thee with a rod, and shall lift up his staff against thee, after the manner of Egypt. For yet a very little while, and the indignation shall cease, and Mine anger in their destruction." We get the manner of this destruction in Isaiah 14:24–25: "The LORD of hosts hath sworn, saying, Surely as I have thought, so shall it came to pass; and as I have purposed, so shall it stand: that I will break the Assyrian in my land, and upon my mountains tread him under foot: then shall his yoke depart from off them, and his burden depart from off their shoulders." It is not to any past destruction of Assyria that these words refer, for this discomfiture is to take place after the restoration of Israel to Palestine in the last days. It will be God's settlement of the so-called Eastern Question.

We learned that this Little Horn will stand up in great wrath against the Jews, "but not [in] his own power" (8:24). He is evidently to have the backing of some more powerful nation, who for selfish purposes will aid him in his nefarious effort to destroy the people of God in that day. In Ezekiel 38–39 we find, I have no doubt, a full account of the power referred to. There we read of "Gog, the chief prince of Meshech and Tubal." Scholars generally are agreed that in place of "chief prince," we should read, "prince of Rosh," and there can hardly be any question that Rosh means Russia. "Gog, the prince of Rosh, Meshech, and Tubal," will evidently be the last czar of all the Russias. Some suppose Meshech and Tubal to be identical with Moscow and Tobolsk, the ancient European and Asiatic capitals of the Slav Empire. It would seem that this ruler will join with the Turkish sultan in opposing the pretensions of the Beast. We can already see events in Europe tending to this. There will be a western and an eastern confederation, and Palestine will be the bone of contention between them.

A fourth figure destined to attract considerable attention in the crisis will be the king of the south, a future ruler of an apparently independent Egypt who, while opposed to Antichrist, nevertheless would seem to act in conjunction with the Beast in opposition to his hereditary enemies the Turks.

In the book of the Revelation the apostle speaks of the drying up of the Euphrates "that the way of the kings of the east [or, from the sun rising] might be prepared" (Rev. 16:12). The drying up of the Euphrates would seem to imply the breaking up of the Turkish power, for as the Nile stands for Egypt so does the Euphrates for the Ottoman Empire. The kings of the sun rising may very well be a descriptive term referring to the nations of the Far East, the "Yellow Peril," dreaded by European statesmen, disputing the possession of the gate to the Orient with the Beast.

If we are thus far correct in our effort to forecast from Scripture the principals in the last great drama of Gentile dominion, we have located an emperor-king of the west, a king of the north, a king of the south, and an alliance of kings of the east, all of whose armies will be marching down upon Palestine at about the same time—Jehovah's land to be the battleground for the fearful Armageddon conflict. Thus Palestine will be exposed to all the horrors and ravages incident to the last premillennial war. It is for this time of horror, little as they realize it, that the Jews from eastern and southern Europe are now returning in large numbers to their ancient home. They are going back that their forefathers' awful prayer may be fully answered, "His blood be on us, and on our children" (Matt. 27:25). Poor, misguided people—the nation of the wandering foot—they fancy that at last a refuge is being provided for them where they will be safe from persecution and secure from danger. But they are really preparing unwittingly for the winepress of the wrath of God from which blood shall flow to the horses' bridles for one thousand six hundred furlongs—the whole actual length of Palestine (Rev. 14:18–20).

After the church has been called away to heaven, there will arise in the city of Jerusalem a man who will present himself to the Jews as the Messiah long promised through the prophets. The apostate part of the nation will at once acknowledge his claims and will say of him, "This is indeed the Messiah for whom we have waited so long; this is the one of whom our Scriptures speak." I judge he will be largely instrumental, in the beginning, in securing them concessions from the Turkish government that they may be established in their land. Afterward he will form a league with the Roman Beast, establishing a covenant between him and the nation for seven years guaranteeing his protection and the integrity of the new Jewish state. Such is the program already outlined by the great Zionist leader Zangwill and the Jewish agitator Max Nordau, who said some time ago, "We are ready to own any man as our Messiah who will establish us again in the land of our fathers."

This will be, I doubt not, exactly what will take place in the coming day. Some great Jew—perhaps he is living now—is going to come to the front who will have much to do in bringing about this restoration. He will be acknowledged by the Western powers as political head of Palestine. He is "the king" of verses 36–39 in our chapter:

And the king shall do according to his will; and he shall exalt himself, and magnify himself above every god, and shall speak marvelous things against the God of gods, and shall prosper till the indignation be accomplished: for that that is determined shall be done. Neither shall he regard the God of his fathers, nor the desire of women, nor regard any god: for he shall magnify himself above all. But in his estate shall he honour the [god] of forces: and a god whom his fathers knew not shall he honour with gold, and silver, and with precious stones, and pleasant things. Thus shall he do in the most strong holds with a strange god whom he shall acknowledge and increase with glory: and he shall cause certain [literal rendering] to rule over many, and shall divide the land for gain.

I now desire to bring to your attention the proofs that the Antichrist must be a Jew living in the land of Palestine with his seat in Jerusalem and who will be acknowledged by the nation of Israel as their Messiah. In doing so, I wish to contrast with this the position of the Roman Catholic pope and point out why, to my mind, he cannot possibly be the one of which is here prophesied, for no pope has ever yet fulfilled these necessary qualifications—nor is there any likelihood that one ever shall. In the first place, it is important to notice that the name Antichrist means simply the false Messiah; that is, he is the one to whom our Lord Jesus Christ referred when He said, "I am come in my Father's name, and ye receive me not: if another shall come in his own name, him ye will receive" (John 5:43). The Antichrist then *is to be received by the Jews*. Has this ever been the case with the popes, or is there any apparent possibility that the Jewish people will ever acknowledge the papacy (which has existed for long centuries) as their Messiah, the hope of their nation? It was to the Jews that Messiah was promised. To them He came in grace, only to be rejected. When the false Messiah comes, they will own *his* claims and hail his advent with joy.

You should not infer from this that Judah alone will be deceived by him. From the second chapter of 2 Thessalonians (a passage we shall be considering later), it is plain that apostate Christendom will also fall into his snare. The Roman Beast will be the civil ruler of the West, while Antichrist will be the religious ruler. The power behind both will be "that old serpent, called the Devil, and Satan" (Rev. 12:9). This will be the anti-trinity—the Devil, the Beast, and the False Prophet. By these will all the nations of the earth be deceived.

Now, as the Jews have never owned the pope as Messiah, neither has any pope made a seven-years' covenant with them, nor yet had his throne in Jerusalem, nor dwelt in the land of Palestine, so it seems clear that there is practically nothing in Scripture to identify the papacy with the Antichrist. Do not misunderstand me and think that I am pleading for the papacy. I believe it to be a most evil thing, but it is not *the* Antichrist.

When he comes, he is to do according to his will and to exalt himself and magnify himself above every god. These gods are undoubtedly the idols of the heathen. But he is also to "speak marvellous things against the God of gods, and . . . neither shall he regard the God of his fathers" (vv. 36–37). Now I submit that only in the wildest hyperbole can such words be applied to the worst of the popes. It is true that some have permitted themselves to be addressed most blasphemously. It is true that a Jesuit writer even dares to speak of "our Lord God the pope." It is likewise true that the pope has been said to have an intimacy with the Father in which even the Lord Jesus Christ does not share. This is based upon the Lord's words to Peter concerning his confession: "Flesh and blood hath not revealed it unto thee, but my Father which is in heaven" (Matt. 16:17). From this, argue the Jesuit sophists, it is evident that the first pope (!) had special illuminations and secrets with the Father in which the Son did not share; and the same privilege, they have declared, belongs to his successors, so that it is safer in some cases to go to the pope than to Christ!

Now all these things, I grant you, are terrible enough. They are horribly blasphemous and must make every truly devout soul shrink in horror from such teaching. But when the last great Antichrist arises, there will be worse even than this. The pope, at least, has never claimed to be above every god. His very title disproves this. He is called the vicegerent of Christ, and he takes the place of being, in a very special sense, God's representative upon the earth. It will be otherwise with the Antichrist. He refuses to own any God. He comes in his own name, and he utterly denies "the God of his fathers." What are we to understand by this last expression? Can it be other than that he is a Jew, and that his fathers after the flesh were Abraham, Isaac, and Jacob? Such is the invariable use of the expression in the Old Testament. I take it as conclusive evidence that the Antichrist is by birth a Jew, but a Jew who has apostatized from the God of his fathers. How could any but a Jew impose upon his nation as being the Messiah when it is clearly predicted in their Scriptures that the Hope of Israel is to spring from the favored nation?

We are also told in verse 37 that he shall not regard "the desire of women, nor regard any god: for he shall magnify himself above all." Now it seems evident that One only can be meant by "the desire of women." Every Jewish woman hoped that it might be the will of God that through her the Messiah would be born into the world. He was emphatically the Desire of women. Antichrist utterly disregards Him, pretending to be himself the predicted One.

But there is a god whom he owns, though evidently a merely natural and human personage. He "shall . . . honour the god of forces: and a god whom his fathers knew not shall he honour with gold, and silver, and with precious stones, and pleasant things" (v. 38). This god can be no other than the Little Horn, the Roman Beast. To him, as we have seen, Antichrist will turn for assistance and support. On his part, he will acknowledge and increase with glory this civil head of the empire, "[causing him] to rule over many" (v. 39) who might not otherwise have owned his sway and dividing with him the land of Palestine for gain. Now I maintain that it is utterly incongruous to attempt to apply all this to the pope, but taken in its natural meaning, all is plain and simple.

From the fortieth verse to the end of the chapter we have a graphic account of the beginning of the conflict of the last days. The king of the south marches against Jerusalem, and the king of the north comes down like a whirlwind with a vast army and navy, entering into the glorious land and the adjacent countries, with the exception of the lands anciently occupied by Edom, Moab, and Ammon. He is at first everywhere triumphant. Egypt is unable to stand against his victorious armies, and he asserts his sway over the land of the Pharaohs, Libya, and Ethiopia. But alarmed by tidings out of the east and the north, he turns back with great fury to meet the powers—doubtless of the Beast and the kings from the sun rising. But upon the mountains of Israel, between the seas, he comes to his end, and none can help him. Thus the last king of the north, the Eastern Little Horn, is finally destroyed. Of Antichrist's destruction we do not here read. That is given us in Revelation 19:20.

Before closing, I wish to link up with this several other Scriptures that add to our knowledge of the false Messiah. In Zechariah 11, after the prophet, personifying the Lord Jesus as the Good Shepherd, is priced at thirty pieces of silver, Zechariah is bidden to take the instruments of a foolish shepherd. "For, lo," says God, "I will raise up a shepherd *in the land*, which shall not visit those that he cut off, neither shall seek the young one, nor heal that that is broken, nor feed that that standeth still: but he shall eat the flesh of the fat, and tear their [hoofs] in pieces. Woe to the idol shepherd that leaveth the flock! the sword shall be upon his arm, and upon his right eye: his arm shall be clean dried up, and his right eye shall be utterly darkened" (vv. 16–17). This idol shepherd is clearly the same as the willful king of our chapter. He is to be raised up in the land—an expression which can refer only to the land of Palestine. He is, beyond a doubt, the one to whom the Lord Jesus was referring in John 5:43

who would come in his own name. The true Shepherd had been rejected; the false one they would receive.

We may now turn to the thirteenth chapter of Revelation. In the first half of the chapter we have the description of the Roman beast. But, beginning with verse 11, we read of another beast coming up out of the earth or land, and he had two horns like a lamb and spoke as a dragon. That is, he looks like and presents himself as the Lamb of God, but his speech is that of the great deceiver of souls. He exercises all the power of the first beast before him, demanding that all worship the first beast. He even does "great wonders, so that he maketh fire come down from heaven on the earth in the sight of men, and deceiveth them" (Rev. 13:13), in order that they may acknowledge the claims of the Beast. He it is who sets up the abomination of desolation, causing men to make an image to the Beast, who all must worship on pain of death. All this is in perfect harmony with what we have learned as to the mutual relationship of the Beast and Antichrist in the book of Daniel. The lamb-like beast comes up from the earth. He is in the land, and his placing "the abomination that maketh desolate" is the signal given by the Lord Jesus for the faithful remnant to flee from Jerusalem.

The signs and wonders by means of which he deceives the world are also mentioned in 2 Thessalonians 2. When laboring in Thessalonica, the apostle had shown them that before the day of the Lord would come, Christ Himself would descend into the air and all His saints would be caught up to meet Him. Of this He reminds them in 1 Thessalonians 4. But it would seem that a report had gotten abroad among them that the day of the Lord had already come, and he writes to correct this. He bids them not to be shaken in their minds, nor fearful in regard to this. For, he tells them, that day could not come until the apostasy had first taken place and the "man of sin [had been] revealed, the son of perdition; who opposeth and exalteth himself above all that is called God, or that is worshipped; so that he as God sitteth in the temple of God, showing himself that he is God" (2 Thess. 2:3–4). But he goes on to speak of a Hinderer, who at the present time is holding back the floodtide of evil. That Hinderer is the presence of the Holy Spirit in the church on earth. At the rapture of the saints, when all the redeemed are caught up to meet the Lord in the air, the Holy Spirit will have returned to heaven.

> *Then* shall that Wicked be revealed, whom the Lord shall consume with the spirit of his mouth, and shall destroy with the brightness of his coming: even him, whose coming is after the working of Satan with all power and signs and lying wonders, and with all deceivableness of unrighteousness

in them that perish; because they received not the love of the truth, that they might be saved. And for this cause God shall send them strong delusion, that they should believe a lie: that they all might be damned who believed not the truth, but had pleasure in unrighteousness. (vv. 8–12)

How perfectly this fits in with the testimony we have been examining in other parts of the Word of God! While the church is on earth, the mystery of lawlessness is already working, but the full revelation of evil cannot be while we are in this scene. When that time comes, we shall be above it all, having been caught up to meet the Lord in the air.

The mystery of lawlessness and the many antichrists of 1 John 2:18 are intimately connected. So here we have a point of agreement with persons who think that the papacy is the Antichrist. We differ with them only as to the use of the article. The papal system is *an* antichrist, and this is true of every system that turns souls away from the truth concerning Christ and His work as the alone ground of salvation. Christian Science is an antichrist, Theosophy is another, Mormonism is another, and so with Spiritism and a host of other ancient and modern cults and fads. The crowning evil of them all is perhaps what is now known as the New Theology, heralded from a thousand pulpits as the finished product of modern thought by men who glory in their freedom from subjection to the Word of God and do not hesitate to brand the Scriptures as a collection of myths and fables, untrustworthy, and less to be relied upon than their own vapid utterances. Every little while someone who has been supposed to be an orthodox Christian preacher comes out with the declaration that he has discovered the unreliability of this or that book of the Bible, and his reckless assertions are received with delight by congregations of Christless, unconverted professors, who are glad to be absolved from allegiance to a book whose teachings make them uneasy in conscience while living for themselves in the world.

If the day ever came that a man who had actually known the Lord Jesus as his own Savior and had enjoyed communion with Him was forced by irresistible evidence to believe that the Bible was not true and the precious gospel story an unreliable tradition of men, do you know what would happen? *It would break his heart.* He would never be found among the shallow, empty religionists of the day, who can complacently acquiesce in the vaporings of the so-called Higher Critics and New Theology preachers. He would be found weeping with Mary and exclaiming in deepest grief, "They have taken away my Lord, and I know not where they have laid Him" (John 20:13).

But it is far otherwise with these unreal professors who drink in so greedily the veneered infidelity that Christless preachers proclaim. What does it do for these men? When they thought the Bible true, it served as a check upon their lawless desires and appetites. They chafed under its restraints. But when the time comes that the whole thing goes out of the window and they become enfranchised, as they call it, they were never so happy in all their life! Ah, I assure you, beloved, people who really have known Christ would feel very differently about having to give up the precious Word of God through which He had been revealed to their souls. You see, such are acquainted with the divine *Person,* the Son of the living God. The others had but a *theory* that they are thankful enough to be rid of.

Those who preach these false gospels are the many antichrists of the present dispensation. When the lawless one himself is revealed, they will be the first to acknowledge his impious claims, deceived by the strong delusion sent from God that all might be judged who received not the love of the truth that they might be saved.

Already it would seem as though that strong delusion were beginning. I know nothing sadder, nothing more lamentable, than the awful power of these evil things that are spreading through Christendom, eating out its very life, like a moral or religious cancer. How seldom you ever see a soul brought back from the awful abyss of Spiritism! How seldom persons are ever recovered from Theosophy or Christian Science! And the reason is plain: there is a satanic power, working in them all that gains absolute control over those who have heard the gospel of God only to refuse and reject it. But, thank God, there are those to whom the words of the apostle apply: "But we are bound to give thanks always to God for you, brethren beloved of the Lord, because God hath from the beginning chosen you to salvation through sanctification of the Spirit and belief of the truth" (2 Thess. 2:13).

God grant that each one that hears these words may thus be manifested as a child of God, born of the Holy Spirit and of the Word, happy in the knowledge of peace made and redemption accomplished through the glorious work of Christ upon the Cross.

THE TIME OF THE END

Daniel 12

This final chapter connects intimately with that which has gone before. "At that time"—that is, at the time of the rise of the Antichrist and the overthrow of the Assyrian or king of the north—"shall Michael stand up, the great prince which standeth for the children of thy [Daniel's] people" (v. 1). There is very likely a close connection here with what we have recorded in the twelfth chapter of the book of Revelation. There John sees war in heaven. The dragon and his angels fight to maintain their place in the upper air, where they may have access to the presence of God that Satan the accuser, or adversary of Zechariah 3, may still resist the Jews—a remnant of whom will have turned to the Lord. But the time having come when God will act openly on their behalf, Michael and his angels are sent to expel the satanic hosts from the heavens. Defeated above, the Devil turns to vent his wrath upon the remnant, the seed of the woman, Israel, who is seen in the beginning of the chapter, and "of whom as concerning the flesh Christ came" (Rom. 9:5). He and His church, together represented in the Man-child, having been caught up to God and to His throne, there will no longer be found on earth any rightfully bearing the name of Christians. But the fullness of the Gentiles having come in, the Jews will be grafted back into their own olive tree, and to them will be committed the testimony for the time of the

125

end. Against this remnant company all the malice of the Devil will be directed: "And there shall be a time of trouble, such as never was since there was a nation even to that same time: and at that time [Daniel's] people shall be delivered [not all who were Jews by natural birth, but], every one that shall be found written in the book" (v. 1). These are they whose names are written in the Book of Life of the slain Lamb from the foundation of the world, and for them the earthly kingdom has been prepared.

Tested by the proclamation of the everlasting gospel on the one hand and the placing of "the abomination that maketh desolate" on the other, there will be a national and religious awakening on the part of those who have so long been sleeping among the dead. The second verse does not, I believe, speak of an actual physical resurrection, but rather of a moral and national one: "Many of them that sleep in the dust of the earth shall awake, some to everlasting life, and some to shame and everlasting contempt." It is the same kind of language that is used both in Isaiah 26:12–19 and Ezekiel 37 to describe Israel's national and spiritual revival. For centuries they have been sleeping in the dust of the earth, buried among the Gentiles. Their awakening will have taken place at last. But while for some it will be to everlasting life and blessing in the glorious kingdom of the Son of Man soon to be established, for the apostates it will be to everlasting shame and contempt because of their submission to the Beast and the Antichrist.

Then shall the wise (that is, the teachers among the remnant, the same class who are referred to in the latter part of verse ten) "shine as the brightness of the firmament; and they that turn many to righteousness as the stars for ever and ever" (v. 3). While these words refer primarily to the faithful of Judah in that day, we also may find encouragement and cheer in them. "He that winneth souls is wise" (Prov. 11:30), or as the Revised Version puts it, "He that is wise winneth souls." May ours be the wisdom that leads us so to walk as to commend the gospel of Christ to all with whom we come in contact, that thus we may be in very deed winners of souls, turning many to righteousness.

Daniel was told to shut up the words and seal the book, even to the time of the end. This is in marked contrast with the message of the angel to the apostle John at the close of the book of Revelation: "And he saith unto me, Seal not the sayings of the prophecy of this book: for the time is at hand" (22:10). The present age or church period is looked at as being but a moment, so to speak, in the ways of God. Messiah having come and been rejected by Israel, the next thing in prophetic order is the time of the end. If this dispensation be lengthened out a little longer, it is but an evidence of God's long-suffering to sinners, being not willing that any should perish, but that all should turn to Him and live (see 2 Peter 3:9).

Throughout the New Testament the end is always looked upon as having drawn nigh. Therefore, through the book of Revelation, the seal is removed, as it were, from the book of Daniel, and the latter prophecy is found to be the key to the former. The fourth verse closes with the statement that "many shall run to and fro, and knowledge shall be increased." Could anything more aptly set forth the chief characteristics of these last days? Men seem to have a perfect mania for traveling from place to place, and human inventions of all kinds are pressed into service to accelerate and make comfortable those who thus run to and fro. Coupled with this we have the ever-widening diffusion of the productions of the press, so that knowledge of all kinds is indeed increased. May we not see in these things one evidence that we have almost reached the special prophetic period denominated as the "time of the end"?

From the fifth verse to the end of our chapter we seem to have a kind of an appendix. The writing of the "Scripture of truth," which the angel began to unfold in the beginning of chapter 11, was concluded in the fourth verse. What follows gives additional light as to times and seasons. The awe-inspiring being described in chapter 10 is still with Daniel, but two other angels appear on the scene also, one standing on each bank of the river. One of these speaks to the man clothed in linen and asks, "How long shall it be to the end of these wonders?" (v. 6). He is evidently referring to the Great Tribulation, and he inquires its actual duration. The answer is given, with great solemnity, that it shall be "for a time, times, and an half; and when he shall have accomplished to scatter the power of the holy people, all these things shall be finished" (v. 7). This agrees with the times given in 7:25, during which the Little Horn was to be permitted to speak great things against the Most High, and to think to change times and laws. At its expiration, the judgment was to sit and his dominion be taken away. This is, of course, the premillennial warrior judgment described in the nineteenth chapter of Revelation. The angel's declaration that "when he shall have accomplished to scatter the power of the holy people, all these things shall be fulfilled" refers undoubtedly to this Little Horn's violent persecution of the remnant to be followed by the manifestation of Messiah.

Daniel tells us that he heard but understood not. Through the book of Revelation we need not be perplexed as he was, for God has now unfolded all this in order that we may more fully enter into His ways. The prophet was told to go his way, "for the words are closed up and sealed till the time of the end" (v. 9). In that time, "many shall be purified, and made white, and tried; but the wicked shall do wickedly: and none of the wicked shall understand; but the wise shall understand" (v. 10).

Two other time prophecies complete the book. The Great Tribulation, we know from other passages, commences when the daily sacrifice shall be taken away and "the abomination that maketh desolate" set up, as foretold in verse 11. This is the verse, and not the thirty-first verse of chapter eleven, to which our Lord refers in His great prophecy in Matthew 24. Now we have just seen that the Tribulation is to last for a time, times, and a half—equivalent to three-and-a-half years, or twelve hundred sixty days. But in this eleventh verse we learn that from the beginning of this tribulation there shall be a thousand two hundred and ninety days. The extra thirty days will, doubtless, be devoted to the purging out of the kingdom of all things that offend and do iniquity, though the Lord will appear, on behalf of the remnant and for the destruction of the Beast and Antichrist, at the expiration of the twelve hundred and sixty days. A longer period yet is given in verse 12: "Blessed is he that waiteth, and cometh to the thousand three hundred and five and thirty days." Some have suggested that this would carry on the time to the celebration of the first millennial Feast of Tabernacles, as in Zechariah 14. At any rate, it clearly points us on to the full establishment of the kingdom in power and glory.

Until then Daniel is told to go his way, but the promise is given him, "Thou shalt rest, and stand in thy lot at the end of the days" (v. 13). It is not likely that the prophet lived very much longer, as he would be an aged man at this time, probably past ninety years and perhaps well on to a century old. Soon he was called from a scene in which he had lived to see many of his own prophecies fulfilled. His life began in the land of Judah. He died an exile, though honored and respected, in the land of the stranger. He held positions of trust and confidence under Nebuchadnezzar, Darius, and possibly Cyrus. He saw the rise and fall of Babylon, the head of gold, and the lion with eagle's wings. He beheld the sudden rise and accession to supreme power of the silver breast and arms—the ferocious bear that raised itself upon one side. During its season of domination, he passed away to rest—not in unconscious sleep, but in Abraham's bosom. He passed away there to wait with all the faithful until the voice of Michael the archangel shall be heard at the coming of the Lord Jesus Christ and our gathering together to Him. For of Old Testament saints it is written that "they without us should not be made perfect" (Heb. 11:40). Answering the assembling shout of the Lord in that hour of triumph, Daniel's body shall rise from its unknown grave in glory and incorruption. He shall take his place with Him for whose sake he had borne reproach so often in his life of faithful devotion to God, and thus he "shall stand in his lot," in the place appointed him after all his works have been manifested at the judgment seat of Christ.

He will behold the rise and destruction of the last Beast, dreadful and terrible, in its ten-horned condition. He will see the once-rejected Stone fall from heaven in judgment upon the feet of the image of "the man of the earth." He will see the Son of Man coming as "a Lamb that looked as though it had been offered in sacrifice" (Rev. 5:6 WEYMOUTH) to receive from the hands of the Ancient of Days the seven-sealed scroll of the title deeds to this world. And among that holy number of crowned priests who prostrate themselves at His feet, none will join more loudly or more understandingly in the song of redemption and glory than the one-time captive who "purposed in his heart that he would not defile himself" (1:8). When the King of kings rides forth, clothed in a vesture dipped in blood, Daniel will follow in his train, an intelligent witness of all His ways in judgment, concerning which he once heard but understood not. In the kingdom of glory to follow, he who of old had stood before kings will stand in the presence of the Prince of the kings of the earth in the lot appointed him.

And in that day, all from the beginning who have esteemed the reproach of Christ greater riches than the treasures of earth—all who have been content to suffer for righteousness' sake—all who have witnessed the good confession—will reign in life with Him who was once upon earth the Arch-sufferer, the most misunderstood of all that noble race "of whom the world was not worthy" (Heb. 11:38).

These things are all written in "the Scripture of truth." The day of their fulfillment is at hand. The Judge stands at the door. Soon the mighty and glorious miracle that will close up this age of grace and introduce the coming hour of trial will be performed by omnipotent power. I refer to the resurrection of the dead in Christ and the translation of the living saints. Not one will be left behind. For God has ordained that just as the Flood of old could not take place until Noah and all his household were safe in the ark, so not one seal of the book to be taken by the Lamb can be broken, not a trumpet blown, not a vial of wrath poured out until all the redeemed of this dispensation, with all the saints of the past, are safely gathered around the Lord in heaven.

Each believer may truthfully use the solemnly precious words of Dr. Bonar as his own:

> I murmur not that now a stranger
> I pass along the smiling earth;
> I know the snare, I dread the danger,
> I hate the haunts, I shun the mirth.

My hopes are passing upward, onward,
    And with my hopes my heart has gone;
Mine eye is turning skyward, sunward,
    Where glory lightens round yon throne.

My spirit seeks its dwelling yonder;
    And faith foredates the joyful day,
When these old skies shall cease to sunder
    The one dear love-linked family.

To light, unchanging and eternal,
    From mists that sadden this bleak waste,
To scenes that smile, forever vernal,
    From winter's blackening leaf I haste.

Earth, what a sorrow lies before thee!
    None like it in the shadowy past;
The sharpest throe that ever tore thee,—
    Even though the briefest and the last.

I see the fair moon veil her lustre,
    I see the sackcloth of the sun;
The shrouding of each starry cluster,
    The threefold woe of earth begun.

I see the shadow of its sunset;
    And wrapt in these the Avenger's form;
I see the Armageddon-onset;
    But I shall be above the storm.

There comes the moaning and the sighing,
    There comes the hot tear's heavy fall,
The thousand agonies of dying;
    But I shall be beyond them all.

The Great Tribulation cannot begin while the members of Christ's body are still upon the earth, for the Lord says to the church of this dispensation, "Because thou hast kept the word of my patience, I also will keep thee from the hour of temptation, which shall come upon all the world, to try them that dwell upon the earth" (Rev. 3:10). This applies to all Christians, for one who does not keep the word of Christ's patience is none of His.

The earthly history of the church will end when "the Lord himself shall descend from heaven with a shout, with the voice of the archangel, and the trump of God: and the dead in Christ shall rise first: then we which are alive and remain shall be caught up together with them in the clouds, to meet the Lord in the air" (1 Thess. 4:16–17). Thenceforth we shall be forever with Him.

But upon our departure to heaven the great clock of prophecy will again begin ticking off the times and seasons. From the people of Israel a remnant will be born again, and, gathered out from the mass, they will become the Lord's witnesses on earth in the time of the end. A beloved brother has likened the course of time to a railroad speedway.[1] Sometimes I have been traveling on the railway on an ordinary way-train, with certain local stops to be made according to schedule. But a special has been sent out behind us, and we have been shunted on to a side track until the special, or the limited express, has gone by. Then the signals direct us to once more get on to the main line and complete our regular course. Israel may be likened to the way-train, running along through the course of the years according to prophecy. But when Messiah appeared and they knew Him not but crucified the Lord of glory (at the expiration of the sixty-nine weeks of chapter 9), they were turned off upon the side-track, and they have been waiting there ever since, while the Special of the dispensation of the grace of God, the limited church express, has been going by. When it has passed on and left the main track clear, God is going to give the signal, and the old Jewish way-train will take to the track again, fulfilling the balance of its schedule according to the seventieth week of the prophecy referred to above. In fact, all the prophecies that have to do with the time of the end.

Those of us who are saved by God's sovereign grace are on the church express and are to be a heavenly people throughout the Millennium and to all eternity. Israel after the flesh are the earthly people, but they have forfeited all title to blessing through disobedience. Still God is determined to carry out His word to give them a place of special privilege on the earth. So He will renew a remnant of them by His Holy Spirit and His Word, and will cleanse them from all filthiness and own them as His own once more. They will have their inheritance here upon the earth, but the church and the Old Testament saints will have theirs in heaven.

So all these dates—the times and the seasons that we have in Daniel and Revelation—have nothing to do with this present period while the church express is going by. They are part of the official schedule for the Jewish way-train and will direct its movements when the limited church train has passed on to glory. There is no timetable issued for the Special. No one can say when it will get by. But I feel very certain that if you want to get aboard you will have to do so soon, for everything points to a change of dispensations very shortly. None are aboard that train save those who have been cleansed from their sins by the precious blood of Christ and sealed with the Holy Spirit of promise. Are *you* certain that you are numbered among them? Do you *know* that you have been born from above and that you are now a possessor of life eternal? You cannot afford to be uncertain in regard to these things. They are too momentous—too solemn and serious—for you to go on from day to day hoping everything will turn out all right in the end when, in reality, everything now is all wrong so far as you are concerned if you are out of Christ—a stranger to the grace of God. What folly to trifle with matters of such grave importance trembling in the balance!

If unsaved, and yet desirous of becoming a Christian, listen to the message my Lord bids me bring to you. He says, "If thou shalt confess with thy mouth the Lord Jesus, and shalt believe in thine heart that God hath raised him from the dead, *thou shalt be saved.* For with the heart man believeth unto righteousness; and with the mouth confession is made unto salvation" (Rom. 10:9–10). Let me couple with this a verse from 1 John: "If we confess our sins, he is faithful and just to forgive us our sins, and to cleanse us from all unrighteousness" (1:9).

Now observe carefully, in these two Scripture passages there are two confessions God is calling upon every soul to make. First, confess your sins to God. Then, confess your Savior to men. Is it not simple? As a poor lost sinner you are invited to come to the God you have sinned against, owning your guilt in His holy presence. When you thus come, He promises full forgiveness based upon the finished work of His beloved Son, who upon the Cross *bore the very sins you confess* and, in your room and stead, endured the judgment due them. Believing this—resting on the testimony of the unchanging Word of God—you can turn to your old friends and former companions and say, "I now own the Lord Jesus Christ as *my* Savior and *my* Lord!" And He declares, "Whosoever therefore shall confess me before men, him will I confess also before my Father which is in heaven. But whosoever shall deny me before men, him will I also deny before my Father which is in heaven" (Matt. 10:32–33). Think of it: confess Christ here, and He will confess you there. Deny Him here, and He will deny you there!

Oh hasten to make the two confessions that will give you title to say, "He hath clothed me with the garments of salvation" (Isa. 61:10). Then, when Daniel stands in his lot at the end of the days, you too will stand in your lot among the redeemed company who will follow the Lamb whithersoever He goes. But if you persist in refusing Christ—if you go on denying His name—and die in your sins, you will have to stand in your lot before His judgment throne to hear the words of doom: "Depart from me, ye cursed, into everlasting fire, prepared for the devil and his angels" (Matt. 25:41), *"I know you not"* (v. 12). Awful words, these! Oh that they may never be spoken to you!

With this I close these studies in the book of Daniel. We have seen, in these lectures, how wonderfully prophecy has been corroborated by human historical records as to the past. Surely it has impressed us with this fact, that not one word that God has spoken shall ever fall to the ground. "He . . . will not call back his words" (Isa. 31:2). All that is written will be fulfilled both as to Israel and the church, as to God's people and the nations, and as to each individual soul, whether saved or lost. "Heaven and earth shall pass away," declared the Lord Jesus, "but my [word *never!*]" (Matt. 24:35; Mark 13:31; Luke 21:33). To keep His Word is to live. To refuse it is to die eternally! Let not Satan persuade any that God will be better than His Word. He will fulfill it to the letter, though man may think otherwise and hope for mercy apart from Christ.

> The man may think that all is well,
>   And every fear be calmed:
> He lives,—he dies,—he wakes in hell,—
>   Not only doomed, but *damned.*

To the Christian, the book of Daniel must ever be a precious and soul-stirring record of the love and care of our gracious God, who always watches over His own for blessing no matter how dark the night and who has given us the sure word of prophecy as a light shining in the gloom, "until the day dawn, and the day star arise in [our] hearts" (2 Peter 1:19).

Appendix A

From a multitude of questions and objections handed to the speaker and answered or replied to when lecturing on this book, a selection of those that might be difficulties to others has here been made, together with abbreviated notes of the answers given. Only those bearing directly on the themes treated in Daniel have been preserved. To go fully into them all would be impossible here. But, where considered necessary, reference is made to helpful works.

Questions and Objections Answered

1. Is it the Antichrist or the Roman Little Horn who will make the seven-years' covenant with the Jews?

Answer: In a sense, both. For while the Little Horn is "the prince that shall come" of chapter 9, the Antichrist will be the representative head of the Jewish nation. They "shall divide the land for gain" (or, a price; 11:39). The covenant would seem to be made between them, the Antichrist acting on behalf of "the many"—a term applied to apostate Judah. Just as "the counsel, or covenant, of peace" is between the Father and the Son (Zech. 6:13), so shall "the covenant of death" be sealed by the Beast and the False Prophet.

2. Was not the placing of the Roman eagles (in the siege of Titus) upon the walls of Jerusalem the abomination of desolation spoken of by Daniel and referred to by our Lord?

Answer: No. For the setting up of "the abomination that maketh desolate" is the beginning of the Great Tribulation, and that does not begin until Antichrist is raised up by Satan to impersonate the Messiah.

3. The Seventh-day Adventists teach that "the cleansing of the sanctuary" refers to Christ's entering the holiest of all in heaven at the end of twenty-three hundred year-days in 1844 to cleanse *it*. Is not this the correct explanation of the passage?

Answer: It is a most wretched perversion of Scripture and in its full character blasphemous beyond expression, as the Adventist sanctuary-theory makes Satan to be the sin-bearer and, thus, the real savior of the penitent! Could anything be more horrible?

Scripture plainly teaches that our Lord having "by himself purged our sins, sat down on the right hand of the Majesty on high" (Heb. 1:3). Of necessity, this implies His immediate entrance into the holiest, for the throne of God is there. "We have such an high priest, who is set on the right hand of the throne of the Majesty in the heavens; a minister of the sanctuary, and of the true tabernacle, which the Lord pitched, and not man" (Heb. 8:1–2). There on God's throne, in the holiest, He has been sitting—not since 1844, but ever since His ascension. And because He is there—and the veil rent—believers are bidden to enter there in spirit, too: "Having therefore, brethren, boldness to enter into the holiest by the blood of Jesus . . . let us draw near" (Heb. 10:19, 22). Think of our being invited to draw near and enter into the holiest, and the Son, our great High Priest, Himself shut out until 1844! Could absurdity be more manifest?

The sanctuary contemplated by Daniel is earthly, and the prophecy has already been fulfilled in twenty-three hundred evening-mornings after Antiochus Epiphanes polluted it by setting up a statue of Jupiter Olympus in the holiest.

4. Does not "He shall think to change times and law" refer to the pope, who changed the Sabbath from Saturday, the seventh day, to Sunday, the first day?

Answer: As noted in lecture 7, there is no reference to the pope in the passage. The pope did not change the Sabbath. He simply acknowledged the special place given to the Lord's Day. The Sabbath is, and always has been, the seventh day and will be kept as such in the Millennium.

The Lord's Day is something very different. It belongs to the present dispensation and commemorates the resurrection of our Savior on the first day of the week. If under law, we are bound to observe the seventh day—the Sabbath; but if under grace, we should gladly devote the first day of the week to the worship and service of the Lord, as much as in us lies.

5.   Why is the name of the great king of Babylon spelled Nebuchadnezzar in Daniel but sometimes Nebuchadrezzar in Jeremiah?

Answer: Ancient, as also modern, names were adapted to the speech of the various countries. Nebuchadnezzar seems to be the Hebraized form of the name. The monuments spell it with an *r,* in place of an *n,* as in parts of Jeremiah.

6.   Will you give the exact dates for the computation of the sixty-nine weeks of years that are supposed to have culminated in the cross of Christ?

Answer: The Scripture says, *"After* threescore and two weeks [together with the seven previously mentioned] shall Messiah be cut off" (Dan. 9:26). Just how soon after is not told us, but able chronologists have shown that sixty-nine sevens of years, of 360 days each, had passed before Christ died. The clearest explanation of the times seems to be that given by Sir Robert Anderson in *The Coming Prince.* He calculates that exactly 483 prophetic years had elapsed on the *day* that Christ rode into Jerusalem as the King predicted by Zechariah.

7.   Why is Belshazzar called "son" and Nebuchadnezzar his "father" if they were not so intimately connected?

Answer: Because in the Semitic languages *son* is commonly used for "descendant" and *father* for "ancestor." Thus the Israelites are sons of Abraham, Isaac, and Jacob. And in the same way, the kings of Judah are called sons of David, though many generations may have intervened.

8.   Does not Ezekiel 45:19–20 refer to the cleansing of the heavenly sanctuary at the end of the twenty-three hundred year-days, as in Daniel 8?

Answer: See reply to question 3. The sanctuary of Ezekiel, as the entire context makes plain, is the millennial temple to be built in the midst of the land of Palestine and hallowed for divine service in the time of the kingdom. From chapter 40 to the end of the book, Ezekiel describes this temple and gives its position and the position of the tribes of Israel to the north and south of it. The verses referred to in the question speak of the special dedication service, when the temple will be ready for the renewal of the priestly service and the memorial sacrifices to be observed in the coming age by the earthly people—very much, I judge, as the Lord's Supper is observed among Christians.

9.   Do you not think it is in heaven that Christ is to reign instead of on or over the earth?

Answer: No. Heaven is never said to be a sphere of Christ's kingdom. The heavens rule over the earth, but we do not read of saints reigning in heaven. When the Bible speaks of reigning with Christ, it implies holding something in check, which must be kept down. A king in a kingdom implies there is something to be repressed. People talk about the saints reigning in heaven, but Scripture never so speaks. The saints are on an equality in heaven; all are children with the Father. But in the kingdom one may have a greater place than another, as the kingdom has to do with rewards for service in this life. "If we suffer [with him], we shall also reign with him" (2 Tim. 2:12).

Notice how Scripture puts it. In the present age, in man's day, the Lord Jesus says, "Blessed are they which are persecuted for righteousness' sake" (Matt. 5:10). In our age, Christ is not manifestly reigning. He is rejected, and we are called upon to suffer with Him because Satan is the god of this age. This is not the time of His power; He is not reigning now, and so righteousness suffers.

In the Millennium, or kingdom period, we read, "A king shall reign in righteousness" (Isa. 32:1). In that day righteousness will not suffer; it will *reign,* that is, all evil will be kept down. But that there will be evil still is evident, for at the end of the Millennium Satan comes up from the bottomless pit and finds a great host ready to follow him, showing that there will be many in the Millennium who will be simply kept under by the power of the King—such as have not been regenerated. People in the Millennium period will need to be born again just as much as they do now.

When we come to the new heavens and the new earth, does righteousness reign then? No. We read, "Look for new heavens and a new earth, wherein *dwelleth* righteousness" (2 Peter 3:13; see also Rev. 21:1). The kingdom will be delivered up to the Father. God will dwell with His people; righteousness will dwell in the new heavens and the new earth. There will never be an enemy throughout eternity to lift up his head against God. Of course, the kingdom of God is forever and ever. That is, He will never surrender His throne or be superseded by any other.

I have gone into this somewhat fully in *The Mysteries of God*. See the chapter on "The Mystery of God Finished."

10.   Might not Daniel have avoided being cast into the den of lions if he had acted according to Matthew 6:6 in making his prayer three times a day? Would he not then have avoided giving offense?

Answer: The prophet acted according to the dispensation in which he lived. The words of the Lord Jesus in Matthew 6:6 have a different application and are a rebuke to hypocritical pretenders to a holiness which they do not possess. In 1 Kings 8, note Solomon's prayer. He requested mercies of the Lord for His people, when driven out of their land, if they should pray "toward this house." Daniel acted accordingly, and evidently with the divine approval.

11.   Does Daniel 7 go on to the day of God of 2 Peter 3? What is the difference between the day of the Lord and the day of God?

Answer: It is the bringing in of the kingdom, or the day of the Lord, that is contemplated in Daniel 7. The day of God is the eternal state. In 2 Peter 3, the two are seen overlapping, as it were, in the last great conflagration, which is the close of the one and the beginning of the other.

12.   Is the seventieth week identical with the Great Tribulation?

Answer: The seventieth week will be a period of tribulation for all the earth dwellers, but it is the last half of the week, or 1,260 days, that is called "the Tribulation, the great one." This will be the season of Antichrist's power and the Beast's war on the remnant.

13.   Will Daniel and the rest of the Old Testament saints be raised with the saints of this dispensation at the time of the Rapture of 1 Thessalonians 4?

Answer: The word is plain: "Christ the firstfruits; afterward *they that are Christ's* at his coming" (1 Cor. 15:23). This includes all saints from Abel to the end of the present age.

14. Will Old Testament saints be manifested with the church at the judgment seat of Christ?

Answer: Surely, else how could Daniel stand in his lot at the time of the end?

Prove all things; hold fast that which is good. (1 Thessalonians 5:21)

Appendix B

OUTLINE of the BOOK of

CHAPTER I: INTRODUCTORY—The MORAL CONDITION suited to EN[...]

TIMES OF THE GENTILES	CHAPTER II	CHAPTER III	CHAPTER IV	CHAPTER V	CHA[...]
	 BABYLON vs. 38. MEDO-PERSIA vs. 39, first clause. GREECE vs. 39, last clause. ROME vs. 40	ENFORCED WORSHIP OF THE IMAGE — A PRESERVED REMNANT Typical of The Abomination of Desolation and the Faithful — Remnant IN	NEBUCHAD-NEZZAR HUMBLED Typical of The Subjugation of all Gentile Power IN	MENE MENE TEKEL UPHARSIN BABYLON DESTROYED MEDO-PERSIA SUCCEEDS TO WORLD EMPIRE Typical of The Impiety And Doom of Gentile Power IN	DA[...] PRE[...] LIO[...] T[...] The [...] Isr[...] Re[...]

The PRESENT AGE or CHURCH P[...]
Revelation of THE MYSTERY. A Date[...]

REVIVED ROMAN EMPIRE IN THE TIME OF THE END.	THE TIME OF THE END MATT. 24: 15-24 REV. 13: 11-18.	THE TIME OF THE END ISA. 60: 12-16	THE TIME OF THE END REV. Chaps. 17-19.	TH[...] OF [...] JER[...] ZEC[...] RE[...]

GENTILE DOMINION ABOLISHED: CHRIST'S KINGDOM E[...]

LOIZEAUX BROTHERS, INC., PUBLISHERS

IEL the **PROPHET** (Matt. 24:15)

NT in the WAYS and COUNSELS of GOD. SEPARATION MAINTAINED. "The Undefiled in the Way"

CHAPTER VII	CHAPTER VIII	CHAPTER IX The PROPHECY of The 70 WEEKS or Heptads of Years	CHAPTERS X, XI, XII PROPHETIC HISTORY IN DETAIL
BABYLON			CHAPTER X: ANGELIC MINISTRY and the "WORLD-RULERS OF THIS DARKNESS" (Eph. 6:12)
MEDO-PERSIA	MEDO-PERSIA	NEH. 2. JERUSALEM REBUILT	CHAPTER XI: 1-3 WORLD-EMPIRE PASSES TO GREECE
GREECE	GREECE	"UNTO MESSIAH THE PRINCE"	VERSES 4-35: WARS OF THE PTOLEMIES AND THE SELEUCIDÆ (EGYPT and SYRIA)
ROME	[ANTIOCHUS DEFILES THE SANCTUARY] THE 2300 DAYS	MESSIAH CUT OFF	

(Chapter IX column side text: 69 Heptads = 483 years to Christ's Coming and Rejection)

D: From the *CROSS* to the *RAPTURE*.

ARENTHESIS in GOD'S GREAT PLAN (EPH. 3: 3-11.)

THE ROMAN LITTLE HORN IN THE TIME OF THE END REV. 13:1-10.	THE GRECIAN LITTLE HORN IN THE TIME OF THE END ISA. 14:24-27.	1 Heptad = 7 yrs. The Time of the End	ANTI-CHRIST'S FALSE COVENANT	CHAPTER XI: 36-45 and XII: ANTICHRIST AND HIS OVERTHROW IN THE TIME OF THE END

SHED RIGHTEOUSNESS TRIUMPHANT. Chap. 7: 13-14.

DESIGNED BY H. A. IRONSIDE

ENDNOTES

Lecture 1: The Needed Moral Condition to Know and Understand God's Mind

1. The RV omits the expression in the last passage noted, though retaining it in Matthew.
2. The definite article will not be found in the KJV of 1 Timothy 1:19, but will be shown in any good critical translation.

Lecture 3: The Abomination of Desolation in Type

1. See the postscript, or dedication, closing the prophecy of Habakkuk.

Lecture 5: Belshazzar's Impious Feast and Overthrow of Babylon

1. Neriglissar and Laborosoarchod, who each reigned but for a brief season after the death of Evil-Merodach, were not of the royal blood.

Lecture 6: The Preservation of the Faithful Remnant in Type

1. H. A. Ironside, *The Mysteries of God* (New York: Loizeaux Brothers, 1946). In this little book I have gone into this somewhat at length.
2. See a pamphlet by J. N. Darby, "What Saints Will Be in the Tribulation?" and another by H. A. Ironside, "Who Will Be Saved in the Coming Period of Judgment?"

Lecture 8: The Grecian Little Horn

1. I am often asked to recommend a good exposition of Revelation. I know nothing better than F. W. Grant, *The Revelation of Jesus Christ* (n.p., n.d.).
2. This was written several years before World War I and the years that followed. What is to result from this fearful conflict remains to be seen.

Lecture 9: The Seventy Weeks

1. The beloved Paul J. Loizeaux, now with Christ, is the brother referred to.

Lecture 10: Angelic Agency

1. It is with the greatest diffidence that I here dissent from the interpretation given by the late W. Kelly and a number of other able expositors. My sole reason for doing so is that given in the text. The careful student might profitably consult William Kelly's *Notes on Daniel* (New York: Loizeaux Brothers, 1952) and weigh what is there stated to this glorious angel. Some do not consider the angel-speaker of verse 11 and following to be the same as the one first described.

2. How solemnly has this been demonstrated in the past five years! I have left the passage in the text as when first written, though at this time there is no longer a czar of Russia.

3. A quotation from a "New Theology" sermon.

Lecture 13: The Time of the End

1. A. E. Booth, to whom I am indebted for this illustration.